volume 2 14 Presentati

the complete guide to
Godly Play

Jerome W. Berryman

An imaginative method for presenting scripture stories to children

TABLE OF CONTENTS

INTRODUCTION

Welcome to *The Complete Guide to Godly Play, Volume 2.* In this volume, we gather together the presentations that form the suggested cycle of lessons for Fall. *Volume 1* of the series, *How to Lead Godly Play Lessons*, provides an in-depth overview of the process and methods of Godly Play. Below, you'll find only quick reminder notes. Please refer to *Volume 1* for an in-depth presentation.

Following this Introduction, you'll find all the information you need to present the lessons of Fall to the children in your Godly Play room. We hope the simple format will enable all teachers, whether new or experienced, to find the information they need to enter fully into the most rewarding play we share: Godly Play.

WHAT IS GODLY PLAY?

Godly Play is what Jerome Berryman calls his interpretation of Montessori religious education. It is an imaginative approach to working with children, an approach that supports, challenges, nourishes and guides their spiritual quest. It is more akin to spiritual direction than to what we generally think of as religious education.

Godly Play assumes that children have some experience of the mystery of the presence of God in their lives, but that they lack the language, permission and understanding to express and enjoy that in our culture. In Godly Play, we enter into parables, silence, sacred stories and sacred liturgy in order to discover God, ourselves, one another and the world around us.

In Godly Play, we prepare a special environment for children to work with adult guides. Two teachers guide the morning session, making time for the children:
- to enter the space and be greeted
- to get ready for the presentation
- to enter into a presentation based on a parable, sacred story or liturgical action
- to respond to the presentation through shared wondering
- to respond to the presentation (or other significant spiritual issue) with their own work, either expressive art or with the lesson materials
- to prepare and share a feast
- to say goodbye and leave the space

To help understand what Godly Play *is*, we can also take a look at what Godly Play is *not*. First, Godly Play is *not* a complete children's program. Christmas pageants, vacation Bible school, children's choirs, children's and youth groups, parent-child retreats, picnics, service opportunities and other components of a full and vibrant children's ministry are all important and are not in competition with Godly Play. What Godly Play contributes to the glorious mix of activities is the heart of the matter, the art of knowing and knowing how to use the language of the Christian people to make meaning about life and death.

Godly Play is different from many other approaches to children's work with scripture. One popular approach is having fun with scripture. That's an approach we might find in many church school pageants, vacation Bible schools or other such suggested children's activities.

Having superficial fun with scripture is fine, but children also need deeply *respectful* experiences with scripture if they are to fully enter into its power. If we leave out the heart of the matter, we risk trivializing the Christian way of life. We also miss the profound fun of existential discovery, a kind of "fun" that keeps us truly alive!

HOW DO YOU DO GODLY PLAY?

When doing Godly Play, *be patient*. With time, your own teaching style, informed by the practices of Godly Play, will emerge. Even if you use another curriculum for church school, you can begin to incorporate aspects of Godly Play into your practice—beginning with elements as simple as the greeting and goodbye.

Pay careful attention to the environment you provide for children. The Godly Play environment is an "open" environment in the sense that children may make genuine choices regarding both the materials they use and the process by which they work toward shared goals. The Godly Play environment is a "boundaried" environment in the sense that children are protected and guided to make constructive choices.

As teachers, we set nurturing boundaries for the Godly Play environment by managing *time, space* and *relationships* in a clear and firm way. The setting needs such limits to be the kind of safe place in which a creative encounter with God can flourish. Let's explore each of these in greater depth.

HOW TO MANAGE TIME

AN IDEAL SESSION

In its research setting, a full Godly Play session takes about two hours. An ideal session has four parts, each part echoing the way most Christians organize their worship together.

OPENING: ENTERING THE SPACE AND BUILDING THE CIRCLE

The storyteller sits in the circle, waiting for the children to enter. The door person helps children and parents separate outside the room, and helps the children slow down as they enter the room. The storyteller helps each child sit in a specific place in the circle, and greets each child warmly by name.

The storyteller, by modeling and direct instruction, helps the children get ready for the day's presentation.

HEARING THE WORD OF GOD: PRESENTATION AND RESPONSE

The storyteller first invites a child to move the hand of the Church "clock" wall hanging to the next block of color. The storyteller then presents the day's lesson. At the presentation's end, the storyteller invites the children to wonder together about the lesson. The storyteller then goes around the circle asking each child to choose work for the day. If necessary, the door person helps children get out their work, either storytelling materials or art supplies. As the children work, some might remain with the storyteller who presents another lesson to them. This smaller group is made up by those who aren't able to choose work on their own yet.

SHARING THE FEAST: PREPARING THE FEAST AND SHARING IT IN HOLY LEISURE

The door person helps three children set out the feast—such as juice, fruit or cookies—for the children to share. Children take turns saying prayers, whether silently or aloud, until the last prayer is said by the storyteller. The children and storyteller share the feast, then clean things up and put the waste in the trash.

DISMISSAL: SAYING GOODBYE AND LEAVING THE SPACE

The children get ready to say goodbye. The door person calls each child by name to say goodbye to the storyteller. The storyteller holds out hands, letting the child make the decision to hug, hold hands or not touch at all. The storyteller says goodbye and reflects on the pleasure of having the child in this community.

In the research setting, the opening, presentation of the lesson and wondering aloud together about the lesson might take about half an hour. The children's response to the lesson through art, retelling and other work might take about an hour. The preparation for the feast, the feast and saying goodbye might take another half an hour.

IF YOU ONLY HAVE THE FAMOUS FORTY-FIVE MINUTE HOUR

You may have a limited time for your sessions—as little as forty-five minutes instead of two hours. With a forty-five-minute session, you have several choices.

FOCUS ON THE FEAST

Sometimes children take especially long to get ready. If you need a full fifteen minutes to build the circle, you can move directly to the feast, leaving time for a leisurely goodbye. You will not shortchange the children. The quality of time and relationships that the children experience within the space *is* the most important lesson presented in a session of Godly Play.

FOCUS ON THE WORD

Most often, you will have time for a single presentation, including time for the children and you to respond to the lesson by wondering together. Finish with the feast and then the goodbye ritual. Because the children will have no time to make a work response, we suggest that every three or four sessions, you omit any presentation and focus on the work instead (see directly below).

FOCUS ON THE WORK

If you usually must pass from the presentation directly to the feast, then every three or four sessions, substitute a work session for a presentation. First build the circle. Then, without making a presentation, help children choose their work for the day. Allow enough time at the end of the session to share the feast and say goodbye.

PLANNING THE CHURCH YEAR

We've simplified annual planning by presenting the lessons in their suggested seasonal order of presentation.

In Fall, an opening session on the Church year is followed by Old Testament stories, from creation through the prophets. In Winter, we present the season of Advent and the Feasts of Christmas and Epiphany, followed by the parables. In spring, we present the faces of Christ during Lent, followed by Easter presentations of the resurrection, the Eucharist and the early Church.

Not all groups will—or should!—follow this suggested order. Some possible exceptions:
- Groups with regularly scheduled short sessions will need to substitute work sessions for presentations every third or fourth Sunday.
- If the storyteller is not yet comfortable with a particular presentation, we recommend substituting a work session for that day's presentation.
- Within a work session, one child might request the repetition of an earlier presentation. Another child might ask a question that draws on an enrichment presentation; for example, "Why do we have crosses in church?" That's a "teachable moment" to bring out the object box of crosses.

HOW TO MANAGE SPACE

GETTING STARTED

We strongly recommend a thorough reading of *The Complete Guide to Godly Play, Volume 1: How to Lead Godly Play Lessons*.

To start, focus on the relationships and actions that are essential to Godly Play, rather than on the materials needed in a fully equipped Godly Place space. We know that not every parish can allocate generous funds for Christian education. We believe Godly Play is worth beginning with the simplest of resources. Without any materials at all, two teachers can make a Godly Play space that greets the children, shares a feast and blesses them goodbye each week.

When Jerome Berryman began his teaching, he used shelving made from boards and cinder blocks, and only one presentation material: figures for the parable of the Good Shepherd, cut from construction paper and placed in a shoe box he had spray-painted gold.

Over the year, Berryman filled the shelves with more homemade lesson materials. When more time and money became available, he upgraded those materials to ones cut from foamcore. Now his research room is fully equipped with the full range of beautiful and lasting Godly Play materials: parable boxes, Noah's ark, a desert box filled with sand. All of these riches are wonderful gifts to the children who spend time there, but the *start* of a successful Godly Play environment is the nurturing of appropriate relationships in a safe space.

MATERIALS

MATERIALS FOR PRESENTATIONS

Each lesson details the materials needed in a section titled "Notes on the Materials." You can make materials yourself, or order beautifully crafted materials from:

Godly Play Resources
P.O. Box 563
Ashland KS 67831
(800) 445-4390
fax: (620) 635-2191
www.godlyplay.com

Here is a list of all suggested materials for the presentations of the Fall quarter:

- *throughout the year (for all or many of the lessons)*
  — Circle of the Church Year (wall hanging)
  — set of crèche figures
  — cloths in liturgical colors (white, purple, red, green)
  — figure of the risen Christ
  — juice, fruit and/or cookies
  — matzo (Lesson 5 and beyond)

- *Orientation Session: Beginning the Godly Play Church School Year*
  — *optional:* handouts

- *Lesson 1: The Circle of the Church Year*
  — Circle of the Church Year (presentation set)

- *Enrichment Lesson: The Holy Family*
  — Holy Family figures
  — figure of the risen Christ
  — cloths in liturgical colors (white, purple, red, green)

- *Lesson 2: Creation*
  — creation cards, black underlay

- *Lesson 3: The Flood and the Ark*
  — ark
  — Noah and Noah's family figures
  — pairs of animals figures
  — dove figure, basket with lid
  — *optional:* prism

- *Lesson 4: The Great Family*
  — desert box
  — Abraham, Sarah, Rebekah, Isaac figures
  — basket of stones
  — blocks for Haran and Ur
  — blue yarn

- *Lesson 5: The Exodus*
  — desert box
  — People of God figures
  — blue felt "water"
  — matzo

- *Lesson 6: The Ten Best Ways*
  — desert box
  — People of God figures
  — heart-shaped box with tablets for the Ten Commandments
  — large rock for Mount Sinai

- *Lesson 7: The Ark and the Tent*
  — desert box
  — ark of the covenant
  — tent and 4 coverings (blue linen, woven goats' hair, red cloth, tanned goatskin)
  — furnishings (incense altar, seven-branched lamp (menorah), table for the 12
    pieces of bread, altar, basin)
  — People of God figures

- *Lesson 8: The Ark and the Temple*
  — temple
  — furnishings (ark of the covenant, incense burner, table for the 12 pieces
    of bread, seven-branched lamp (menorah), altar, basin)
  — Solomon figure
  — scroll

- *Lesson 9: The Exile and Return*
  — desert box
  — People of God figures
  — heavy chain
  — blue yarn
  — blocks for Haran and Babylon

- *Enrichment Lesson: The Prophets*
  — desert box
  — People of God figures
  — chain
  — blue yarn
  — blocks for Haran and Babylon
  — 4 scrolls

- *Enrichment Lesson: Jonah, the Backward Prophet*
  — boat
  — Nineveh model or block
  — Jonah figure
  — felt (blue "water," brown "land")
  — green "vine"
  — blue sea-strips (waves)

- *Enrichment Lesson: The Books of the Bible*
  — wooden bookshelf with wooden "books" of the Bible
  — Bible on stand

MATERIALS FOR CHILDREN'S WORK

Gather art supplies that the children can use to make their responses. These materials are kept on the art shelves. We suggest:
- paper
- painting trays
- paint and brushes
- drawing boards
- crayons, pencils and markers
- boards for modeling clay
- clay rolled into small balls in airtight containers

MATERIALS FOR THE FEAST

- napkins
- serving basket
- cups
- tray
- pitcher

MATERIALS FOR CLEANUP

Gather cleaning materials that the children can use to clean up after their work and use to care for their environment. We suggest:
- paper towels
- feather duster
- brush and dustpan
- cleaning cloths
- spray bottles with water
- trash can with liner

HOW TO ARRANGE MATERIALS

The materials are arranged to communicate visually and silently the language system of the Christian faith: our sacred stories, parables and our liturgical action. Main presentations are generally kept on the top shelves.

Enrichment presentations are generally kept on the second shelves. Bottom shelves are kept free for supplemental materials, such as books, maps or other resources. Separate shelves hold supplies for art, cleanup and the feast. A shelf for children's work in progress is also very important.

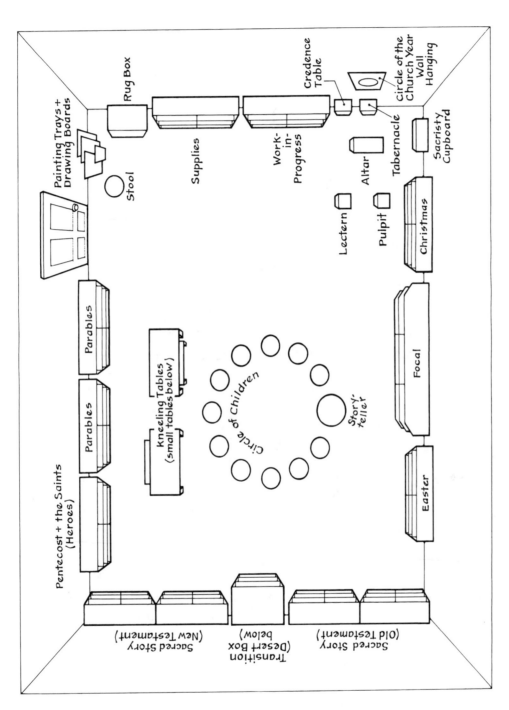

WHERE TO FIND MATERIALS

HOW TO MANAGE RELATIONSHIPS

THE TWO TEACHING ROLES:
DOOR PERSON AND STORYTELLER

Each teaching role fosters respect for the children and the Godly Play space. For example, parents are left at the threshold of the Godly Play space and teachers remain at the children's eye level. Both practices keep the room child-centered, instead of adult-centered.

Similarly when the storyteller presents a lesson, he or she keeps eye focus on the materials of the lesson—not the children. Instead of being encouraged to respond to a teacher, the children are invited, by the storyteller's eyes, to enter the story.

In a typical Sunday morning session, only two adults will be present in the Godly Play space: the door person and the storyteller. These are their respective tasks during a typical session:

DOOR PERSON

Check the shelves, especially the supply shelves and art shelves.

Get out the roll book, review notes and get ready to greet the children and parents.

Slow down the children coming into the room. You may need to take and put aside toys, books and other distracting objects. Help them to get ready. Take the roll or have the older children check themselves in.

Close the door when it is time. Be ready to work with latecomers and children who come to you from the circle.

Avoid casual eye contact with the story-teller to help prevent the adults in the room from turning the children into objects, talking down to them or manipulating them.

STORYTELLER

Check the material to be presented that day.

Get seated on the floor in the circle and prepare to greet the children.

Guide the children to places in the circle where they will best be able to attend to the lesson. Visit quietly until it is time to begin and all are ready.

Present the lesson. Model how to "enter" the material.

Draw the children into the lesson by your introduction. Bring your gaze down to focus on the material when you begin the actual lesson. Look up when the wondering begins.

DOOR PERSON

When the children choose their work, listen so that you can help them get out their work. They need help setting up artwork and getting materials from the shelves for work on a lesson, either alone or in a group.

Stay in your chair unless children need your help. Do not intrude on the community of children. Stay at the eye level of the children whenever possible, as if there is a glass ceiling in the room at the level of the taller children.

Help the children put their work away, and also help the children who are getting ready to lay out the feast.

Sit quietly in your chair, but be sure that the trash can has a liner in it.

Greet the parents and begin to call the names of the children who are ready and whose parents are there.

If a child starts for the door without saying goodbye to the storyteller, remind him or her to return to the storyteller to say goodbye.

STORYTELLER

After the lesson and wondering, go around the circle, dismissing each child to begin his or her work, one at a time. Each child chooses what to do. Go quickly around the circle the first time, returning to the children who did not decide. Go around the circle for decisions until only a few are left—who may be new or for some other reason cannot make a choice. Present a lesson to these children.

Remain seated in the circle unless children need help with the lessons they have gotten out. You may need to help with art materials. Keep yourself at the children's eye level when you help.

When it is time for the feast, go to the light switch and turn it off. Ask the children to put their work away and come back to the circle for the feast. Turn the light back on. Go to the circle to anchor it as the children finish their work and return.

Ask for prayers, but do not pressure. After the feast, show the children how to put their things away in the trash.

Help the children get ready to have their names called.

As the children's names are called, they come to you. Hold out your hands. Children can take your hands, give a hug or keep their distance, as they like. Tell them quietly and privately how glad you were to see them and what good work they did today. Invite them to come back when they can.

DOOR PERSON

Remember to give back anything that may have been taken at the beginning of class.

When the children are gone, check and clean the art and supply shelves.

Sit quietly and contemplate the class as a whole.

Evaluate, make notes and discuss the class with your coteacher.

STORYTELLER

Take time to enjoy saying goodbye, with all the warmth of a blessing for each child.

When all are gone, check the material shelves and clean.

Sit quietly and contemplate the session as a whole.

Evaluate the session, record your notes and discuss the session with your coteacher.

HOW OTHERS CAN HELP

Other adults who want to support the work of a Godly Play space can contribute by:
- taking turns providing festive and healthy food for the children to share during their feasts
- keeping the art and supply shelves replenished with fresh materials
- using their creative skills to make materials for Godly Play presentations

HOW TO RESPOND EFFECTIVELY TO DISRUPTIONS IN THE CIRCLE

You always want to model the behavior you expect in the circle: focused on the lesson and respectful of everyone in the circle. If a disruption occurs, you deal with that disruption in such a way that you still show continual respect for everyone in the circle—including the child who is having trouble that day. You also still maintain as much focus on the lesson as you can, returning to complete focus on the lesson as quickly as possible.

Therefore, as you consider responses, remember to keep a neutral tone in your voice. Remember, too, that our goal is to help the child move himself or herself toward more appropriate behavior. At the first level of interruption, you might simply raise your eyes from the material. You look up, but not directly at the child, while saying, "We need to get ready again. Watch. This is how we get ready." Model the way to get ready and begin again the presentation where you left off.

If the interruption continues or increases, address the child directly. "No, that's not fair. Look at all these children who are listening. They are ready. You need to be ready, too. Let's try again. Good. That's the way."

If the interruption continues or increases, ask the child to sit by the door person. Don't think of this as a punishment or as an exclusion from the story: some children *want* to sit by the door person for their own reasons. Continue to keep a neutral tone of voice as you say, "I think you need to sit by Ann. *(Use the door person's name.)* You can see and hear from there. The lesson is still for you."

The goal is for the child to take himself or herself to the door. If the child is having trouble, or says, "No!", you can say, "May I help you?" Only if necessary do you gently pick up the child or, in some similar way, help him or her go to the door person.

HOW TO SUPPORT THE CHILDREN'S WORK

Show respect for the children's work in two key ways: through the structure of the classroom in which the children work and the language you use—and do *not* use— in talking about their work. Let's explore each of these.

CLASSROOM STRUCTURE

A Godly Play classroom is structured to support children's work in four ways:

- First, it makes *materials* inviting and available by keeping the room open, clean and well-organized. A useful phrase for a Godly Play room is, "This material is for you. You can touch this and work with this when you want to. If you haven't had the lesson, ask one of the other children or the storyteller to show it to you." Children walking into a Godly Play classroom take delight at all the fascinating materials calling out to them. These materials say, "This room is for you."
- Second, it encourages responsible *stewardship* of the shared materials by helping children learn to take care of the room themselves. When something spills, we could quickly wipe it up ourselves, of course. Instead, by helping children learn to take care of their own spills, we communicate to them the respect we have for their own problem-solving capabilities. At the end of work time, each child learns to put away materials carefully. In fact, some children may want to choose cleaning work—dusting or watering plants—for their entire response time.
- Third, it provides a respectful *place* for children's work by reserving space in the room for ongoing or finished projects. When a child is still working on a project at the end of work time, reassure him or her by saying, "This project will be here for you next week. You can take as many weeks as you need to finish it. We never lose work in a Godly Play room." Sometimes children want to give a finished piece of work to the room. Sometimes children want to take either finished or unfinished work home. These choices are theirs to make, and ours to respect.
- Fourth, it sets a leisurely *pace* that allows children to engage deeply in their chosen responses. This is why it's better to do no more than build the circle, share a feast and lovingly say goodbye when we are pressed for time rather than rush through a

story and time of art response. When we tell a story, we want to allow enough time for leisurely wondering together. When we provide work time, we want to allow enough time for children to become deeply engaged in their work. In their wondering or their work, children may be dealing with deep issues—issues that matter as much as life and death. Provide them a nourishing space filled with safe *time* for this deep work.

USING LANGUAGE

You can also support children with the language you use:

- Choose *"open" responses*. We choose "open" responses when we simply describe what we see, rather than evaluate the children or their work. Open responses invite children's interaction, but respect children's choices to simply keep working in silence, too. *Examples:*
  — Hm. Lots of red.
  — This is big work. The paint goes all the way from here to there.
  — This clay looks so smooth and thin now.
- Avoid *evaluative responses.* Evaluative responses shift the child's focus from his or her work to your praise. In a Godly Play classroom, we want to allow children the freedom to work on what matters most to them, not for the reward of our praise. *Examples:*
  — You're a wonderful painter.
  — This is a great picture.
  — I'm so pleased with what you did.
- Choose *empowering responses*, which emphasize each child's ability to make choices, solve problems and articulate needs. In a Godly Play classroom, a frequently heard phrase is, "That's the way. You can do this." We encourage children to choose their own work, get the materials out carefully and clean up their work areas when they are done. When a child spills something, respond with, "That's no problem. Do you know where the cleanup supplies are kept?" If a child needs help, show where the supplies are kept or how to wring out a sponge. When helping, the aim is to restore ownership of the problem or situation to the child as soon as possible.
- Stay alert to the children's *needs* during work and cleanup time. The door person's role is especially important as children get out and put away their work. By staying alert to the children's choices in the circle, the door person can know when to help a new child learn the routine for using clay, when a child might need help moving the desert box or when a child might need support in putting material away or cleaning up after painting.

MORE INFORMATION ON GODLY PLAY

The Complete Guide to Godly Play, Volumes 1-4 by Jerome Berryman are available from Living the Good News (Denver, 2002). *Volume 1: How To Lead Godly Play Lessons* is the essential handbook for using Godly Play in church school or a wide variety of alternative settings. *Volumes 2-4* present complete presentations for Fall, Winter and Spring.

The *Center for the Theology of Childhood* is the nonprofit organization that sponsors ongoing research, training, accreditation programs, the development of a theology of childhood for adults and support of Godly Play. The Center maintains a schedule of training and speaking events related to Godly Play, as well as a list of trainers available throughout this and other countries for help in establishing Godly Play programs.

Contact information:

Center for the Theology of Childhood at Christ Cathedral
1117 Texas Avenue
Houston TX 77002
(713) 223-4305
fax: (713) 223-1041
e-mail: theologychild2@earthlink.net
www.godlyplay.net

Godly Play Resources crafts beautiful and lasting materials especially for use in a Godly Play classroom. Although you can make your own materials, many teachers find their work both simplified and enriched by using Godly Play Resources to supply their classrooms. *Contact information:*

Godly Play Resources
P.O. Box 563
Ashland KS 67831
(800) 445-4390
fax: (620) 635-2191
www.godlyplay.com

BEGINNING THE GODLY PLAY CHURCH SCHOOL YEAR

OPENING CELEBRATION AND ORIENTATION

We suggest you begin a Godly Play year by gathering the whole Sunday school together on the first Sunday of your education program. In your hall or other community space, set up one table per classroom. The pair of coteachers for each classroom can sit at their assigned table to meet the children and their parents.

OPENING

Provide an extra table near the entrance for session hosts, who can "direct traffic" to the appropriate class tables. In addition to meeting children and parents, teachers can give families useful handouts for the church school year. *Examples:*

- a schedule of Godly Play sessions (Handing out refrigerator magnets with these would be a nice touch.)
- "The Ten Best Ways for Parents"
- parent education schedule (This should include times for the Godly Play Parent Sessions described below.)
- guide to your church's complete program for children and families (Godly Play is not a complete program; emphasize this fact by providing information on children's choirs, vacation Bible schools, family nights, annual pageants and so on.)

FEAST AND ROOM VISITS

After children and parents meet the teachers, they can share conversation, a simple snack and beverages—a beginning "feast" to celebrate our church year together. Once all the parents have arrived, teachers should feel free to mingle.

Teachers leave the celebration a few minutes before parents to go the classrooms. Parents can then have the opportunity to tour the classrooms at the end of this orientation session. Children who have been in Godly Play rooms before will often want to act as tour guides for their parents: "This is where we keep the clay!"

FOLLOW-UP TO THE OPENING DAY FOR PARENTS: GODLY PLAY PARENT SESSIONS

Parents naturally want to know what goes on during a Godly Play lesson. Welcome this opportunity to invite parents into the Godly Play experience. For each session, you will need to provide alternative space, leaders and activities for the children, so that their parents can fully enjoy together the Godly Play room. We suggest that you offer these sessions first to the parents of the youngest children, then work your way up to classes of older children.

In your invitation to parents, explain that they will experience a full Godly Play session: building the circle, hearing the lesson, responding with art or play, sharing a feast and saying goodbye. Emphasize in your invitation to parents that they need not—and should not—roleplay the parts of children during this time. They can also sit in chairs, if they wish, and not on the floor. This is their opportunity to experience, as adults, exactly what happens during a Godly Play session. You can make time available after the session to answer parents' questions about the experience they have shared.

SAMPLE HANDOUT

THE TEN BEST WAYS FOR PARENTS

One Godly Play lesson tells children about the "Ten Best Ways" to live. This is the story of the Ten Commandments that God gave to God's People.

Here we offer "Ten Best Ways" for parents—not commandments, but ways we invite you, the parent, to share more fully in your child's Godly Play experience.

Godly Play, Jerome Berryman's interpretation of Montessori religious education, is an imaginative approach to working with children. This approach supports, challenges, nourishes and helps guide their spiritual quest.

Godly Play assumes that children have some experience of the mystery of the presence of God in their lives, but that they lack the language, the permission and the understanding to express and enjoy that spiritual experience in our secular culture. In Godly Play, we enter into our parables, sacred stories, silence and liturgy in order to discover God, ourselves, one another and the world around us.

THE TEN BEST WAYS FOR PARENTS

- Godly Play sessions take place on *(days and dates)* from *(starting time)* to *(ending time)*.
- Please help your children be on time. They won't want to miss a minute!
- The Godly Play circle is built slowly and lovingly, to welcome each child, one at a time. When children arrive, they wait outside the door while the teacher helps them get ready to join the circle.
- Please say your goodbyes at the door, and know that the teachers are ready to make the next hour a safe and welcoming time for every child.

- When you pick up your child, keep in mind that young children will not always be able to tell you what they learned, because what they learned was *how* to learn about the powerful language of the Christian people.
- Also keep in mind that children will not always be able to show you a physical product for their "work" that day, because some of what they've learned cannot be put into words even by adults. In Godly Play, we focus on our relationship with God and the depths of relationships in the community of children.
- Please don't come into the room during class because we want the Godly Play room to be a special place for the community of children. Even the teachers keep their profiles low during a Godly Play session!
- We would be happy to welcome you on a visit to the Godly Play room outside of session time. Call us at *(phone number)* to arrange a visit or to ask any questions you might have about the program.
- We welcome volunteers to support the teachers and the community of children by preparing the weekly "feast," by taking care of the classrooms and materials and by making materials for teachers to use. Call *(phone number)* for more information.
- We hope you will attend a parent orientation class on *(date)*, at *(time)*. This is your chance to experience the Godly Play environment and process together with other parents.

LESSON 1

THE CIRCLE OF THE CHURCH YEAR

LESSON NOTES

FOCUS: HOW THE CHURCH TELLS TIME

- LITURGICAL ACTION
- CORE PRESENTATION

THE MATERIAL

- LOCATION: FOCAL SHELVES
- PIECES: CIRCLE OF THE CHURCH YEAR WALL HANGING, CIRCLE OF THE CHURCH YEAR PRESENTATION SET
- UNDERLAY: USE A SOLID-COLORED RUG

BACKGROUND

This lesson sets the context for the whole year. Each year, the Christian people move through a circle of memory and expectation to open themselves to the elusive presence of God. In the Godly Play classroom, we pay attention to this circle of movement each week.

This lesson uses the Circle of the Church Year presentation set (illustrated on p. 27), which includes a circular frame, fifty-two removable colored blocks and a gold cord or ribbon.

You'll also use the Circle of the Church Year wall hanging (illustrated on p. 24), which has colored cloth "blocks" for the Sundays of the year and a golden arrow that moves from Sunday to Sunday. From now on, begin each class by inviting a child to go to this wall hanging and move the golden arrow to the next Sunday. (Check the wall hanging before class to make sure that when the child moves the arrow to the next block, it will point to the right color.) This invites children to move through the Church's special kind of time, marked not by numbers but by blocks of color.

NOTES ON THE MATERIAL

The Circle of the Church Year presentation set is a circle about one foot in diameter made from wood, poster board, foamcore or felt. Blocks made from the same material fit in a ring to mark each week of the liturgical year, as well as the day of Christmas.

Three arrow-shaped hands of this "clock" point to the three great times of the Church year. If you buy only one ready-made material, we recommend that it be this one. Accurately cutting out these blocks is a difficult job!

This material can either be kept inside a box or set plainly on the shelf. A box adds to the mystery; without a box, children can see the material better when they look around the room. Some sets, intended for older children, include inserts that fit inside the circle. These inserts are labeled with the names of the seasons, months, phases of the moon, etc., so a child can actually find the date of Easter for any given year.

You will use the gold cord or ribbon (about three feet long) to show how time can be "in a line." this cord needs to be flexible and small enough to curl up inside your fist.

Traditions about the use of color for feast days or liturgical seasons vary greatly, even within denominations. As you order the material or prepare this lesson, please adjust as needed to match the colors actually used in your church.

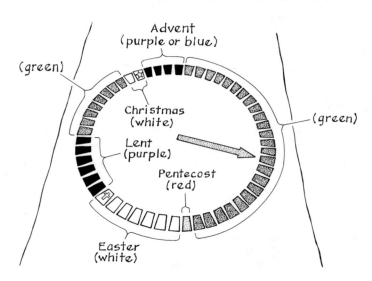

CIRCLE OF THE CHURCH YEAR WALL HANGING

SPECIAL NOTES

Art Project: Although we rarely suggest specific art projects, children might enjoy making their own Circle of the Church Year to take home. Cut out two circles to match the inside and outside diameters of the presentation material's circular slot. The children use these to trace their own circles. They then glue "blocks" made from construction paper between the two lines, using the wall hanging or presentation material for their guide. Finally, they attach the golden arrow to the center of the circle. The individual precut, colored blocks and the arrows and brads for attaching them are kept in their own clear plastic containers. All materials are kept together on a tray. Invite children to take their completed circles with them, so they can follow the Circle of the Church Year at home, the way they do in class.

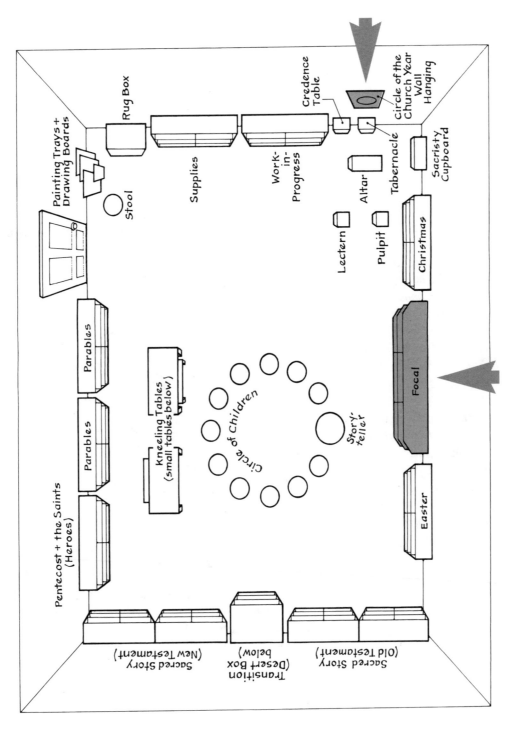

WHERE TO FIND MATERIALS

MOVEMENTS

Get up from your position in the circle and carefully cross the room to the rug box. Pick up a rug with attentive care.

Bring the rug to the circle and roll it out just as carefully and lovingly as you would like the children to do. This is especially important for children younger than eight years old.

The Circle of the Church Year material is usually kept right behind the story teller, so why walk around the room? Reaching back and pulling it off the shelf isn't dramatic enough to catch the children's attention and help them remember where to find the story. Instead, get up and walk around the room until you come back to where the circle sits on its shelf.

Sit down in the circle with the rug in front of you. Place the material to your side. As you do so, pick up the gold cord and enclose it in your hand so that you can pull it out through a space between two fingers. Keep eye contact with the children as you hide the cord in your hand and begin the story.

Until now, the gold cord has been hidden. But now you show a small end of the cord extending between your fingers, and you suddenly notice it.

WORDS

⟶ Now watch carefully. Here is the rug you need for this lesson.

⟶ Watch where I go now to get the lesson.

⟶ Hm. It's not where the sacred stories are. It's not where the parables are. Ah, here it is! This is the lesson about the Circle of the Church Year.

Time, time, time. There are all kinds of time. There is a time to get up in the morning. There is a time to go to bed. There is a time to go to school and a time to come home. There is a time to work, and there is a time to play. But what is time?

⟶ Some people say that time is in a line, but I wonder what that would look like? Ah. Wait a minute. What is this?

MOVEMENTS

Pull out the cord slowly as you speak. Pull it all the way out from your fist slowly as you talk until it drops to the rug.

The end of the cord drops.

Pick up the cord and look at it.

Hold the two ends and look at them.

Tie the two ends (beginnings) together. Then put the circle of wooden blocks on the rug and place the golden circle of time around the circle of the material.

WORDS

Time. Time in a line. This is time in a line. Look at this. Here is the beginning. It is the newest part. It is just being born. It is brand new. Now look.

Look. It is getting older. The part that was new is now getting old. I wonder how long time goes. Does it go forever? Could there ever be an ending?

It ended. Look at the ending.

The beginning that was so new at the beginning now is old. The ending is the new part now. We have a beginning that is like an ending and an ending that is like a beginning.

Do you know what the Church did? They tied the ending that was like a beginning, and the beginning that was like an ending together, so we would always remember that for every ending there is a beginning and for every beginning there is an ending.

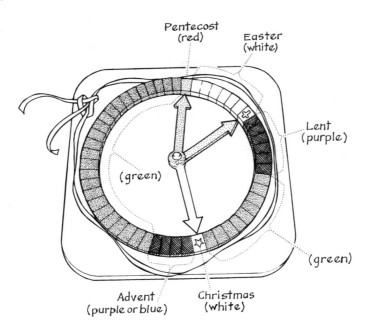

Pentecost (red)

Easter (white)

Lent (purple)

(green)

(green)

Christmas (white)

Advent (purple or blue)

CIRCLE OF THE CHURCH YEAR PRESENTATION SET (STORYTELLER'S PERSPECTIVE)

MOVEMENTS

Leave the golden cord on the material and begin to remove the blocks. Begin with the "three great times" (a white Christmas block, a white Easter block and a red Pentecost block). When you pick up the red Pentecost block, drop it briefly: it's so hot! Remember to speak of the three great "times," since Christmas is not always on a Sunday.

Sit back for a moment and look at the blocks for the three great times.

Place the four purple (or blue) blocks of Advent in a line to your right of the white block for Christmas. Place the six purple blocks for Lent in a line to your right of the white block for Easter.

Touch first the four blocks of Advent, then the six blocks of Lent.

Count out six more white Sunday blocks for the season of Easter and place them to your right of the red block for Pentecost.

Touch Pentecost again, but snatch your hand away because it's still hot.

Now only green blocks are left in the circle. Begin to remove them in groups of three, and place them on the rug in groups of three. Refer to the diagram for correct placement. Pace yourself: you don't want to rush, but you do want to get the blocks out before the children lose interest.

WORDS

Here are the three great times. This is Christmas. This is Easter. This is—ouch! That's hot! This is Pentecost.

People can walk right through these mysteries each year, and not even know what's there. We need time to get ready to come close to these mysteries.

Here are the times for getting ready. The time for getting ready to come close to the mystery of Christmas is called "Advent." The time for getting ready to come close to the mystery of Easter is called "Lent."

Look. The time for getting ready to come close to the mystery of Easter is longer than the time for getting ready to come close to the mystery of Christmas. This is because Easter is an even greater mystery than Christmas.

It is so great that it keeps on going. You can't keep it in one Sunday. It overflows and goes on for six more Sundays. It makes a whole season!

The season of Easter is also a time for getting ready to come close to the mystery of Pentecost. Ouch! It's still hot.

Here are all of the great, green Sundays of the year.

MOVEMENTS **WORDS**

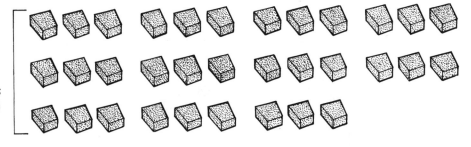

Great,
Green,
Growing
Sundays
(green)

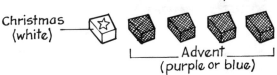

Pentecost
(red)

— Easter (white) —

Easter
(white)

— Lent (purple) —

Christmas
(white)

Advent
(purple or blue)

ALL THE BLOCKS OUT OF THE CIRCLE (STORYTELLER'S PERSPECTIVE)

Now let's see if we can build the circle of the year again. Watch carefully, because the Church tells time by colors as well as by clocks.

Place the white block for Christmas in the empty circle, then the white Easter block and finally the red Pentecost block.

Here are the three great times.

Ouch, it's still hot.

Put the blocks in their approximate final spaces but slide them around to show that those places are not yet set.

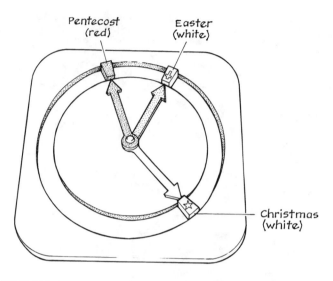

| MOVEMENTS | WORDS |

THE THREE GREAT TIMES IN THE CIRCLE (STORYTELLER'S PERSPECTIVE)

Place the four purple (or blue) blocks for Advent in front of the white Christmas block. Touch each block in turn as you count one, two, three, four.

The time for getting ready for the mystery of Christmas is called Advent. It is one, two, three, four weeks long. The Church year begins with the beginning of Advent.

Sometimes the color for getting ready for Christmas is purple. That's a serious color, the color of kings. Sometimes the color is blue. Do you know why? Because it's one of the colors for the Mother Mary. Without the Mother Mary, there would be no baby Jesus.

Place the six purple blocks for Lent in front of the white Easter block.

The time for getting ready for Easter is usually purple. Purple is the color of kings, and something is going to happen to Jesus, the King. But he was not the kind of king that people thought was coming. He was a different kind of king.

Touch each of the purple Lent blocks in turn as you count one, two, three, four, five, six.

Look, there are one, two, three, four, five, six weeks for getting ready for Easter. It is an even greater mystery than Christmas, so it takes longer to get ready to enter it.

Place the six white blocks for the season of Easter after the block for Easter itself. Touch each block as you count one, two, three, four, five, six.

Easter is so great a mystery that you can't keep it in only one Sunday. It keeps on going for one, two, three, four, five, six weeks.

During that time people met Jesus in a new way. He had died on the cross, and that was very sad. But they kept meeting him.

MOVEMENTS	WORDS

WORDS

Somehow Jesus was still with them, as he is still with us.

Then something wonderful happened. The Apostles went outside of Jerusalem with Jesus in this new way.

Put your two hands over the circle like a blessing. Raise them together about 12".

There they saw him go up.

Move one hand back down and touch the Pentecost block.

And a few days later the Holy Spirit came down. The Church was born. The Apostles glowed with the power of the Holy Spirit. Their tongues were like fire when they spoke. They were more alive than they had ever been before. That's why the color of Pentecost is red like fire.

Begin to put the green blocks into the circle, three at a time. First place nine green blocks between the white Christmas block and the first purple block of Lent.

First we will put in the great, green, growing Sundays between Christmas and the beginning of Lent. The most you can ever have here are nine, so we will put in nine green growing weeks here.

Next place the remaining green blocks, three at a time, between the red Pentecost block and the first purple block of Advent. Take your time and let the children's year unfold in their imaginations as you replace these great, green Sundays.

Here are the rest of the great, green, growing Sundays. Do you know what the Sundays after Pentecost are called? They are called "the Sundays after Pentecost."

Here is the time when school is out. The summer comes and the days get longer and longer. You can play outside later. People go swimming. Some go to camp. Many go on vacation. Then summer comes to an end.

Now you begin to get ready for school. You need new clothes and books. School begins and you often have a new teacher. The days get shorter. School goes on and you get used to all the new things.

Now the days are really short. It gets dark very early. It looks as if the light is just about to go out. Right at that time, when the light seems to be coming to an end, we reach Advent. The year ends, and it begins again. It is time to get ready to enter the mystery of Christmas.

MOVEMENTS	WORDS

MOVEMENTS

These can be shown by the "clock hands" that extend from the middle of the circle to the Christmas, Easter and Pentecost blocks.

If you have inserts that fit inside the circle to label the seasons, you can name the seasons once again as you put the inserts in. These pieces should be cut to the exact length of each area's name, so that older children can check their own work when using this material. If you don't have these inserts, simply touch the blocks named.

Move your hand around the reassembled circle.

Sit back and enjoy the whole circle of beautiful colors. Now it's time to begin the wondering.

These last wondering questions are especially intended to prepare children for a visit to the sacristy, with its mysterious cupboards and wonderful drawers of colors. If possible, arrange for such a visit in the next week or so.

WORDS

Here are the three great times: Christmas. Easter. Pentecost.

Here are the times for getting ready. Advent. That's four weeks. Lent. That's six weeks. You can't keep Easter to just one Sunday, so it keeps on for six more weeks. Those weeks are called the season of Easter, too. Here are the great, green, growing Sundays of the year.

It is all here. Everything we need. For every beginning there is an ending, and for every ending there is a beginning. It goes on and on, forever and ever.

I wonder which one of these colors you like best?

I wonder how the colors make you feel?

I wonder which color is the most important?

I wonder if you have ever seen these colors in the church?

Some of the colors in the church change, and some do not. I wonder where the ones are that change?

I wonder if you have ever come close to these colors in the church?

I wonder what happens in the church when you see these colors?

I wonder who changes the colors there?

I wonder where the colors go when you do not see them?

I wonder why the Church tells time with colors?

MOVEMENTS

Model how you want the children to put the materials away by walking carefully around the circle, carrying the materials with two hands. Return them to the shelf. Then carefully roll up the rug and return it to the rug box.

Begin helping the children decide on their responses. Today you can include the possibility of children making their own circles to take home. See the Special Notes (p. 24) for details.

You might also have a page from a calendar mounted on foamcore to lay beside the circle when you wonder why the Church tells time with colors.

WORDS

Now watch carefully where I go to put this lesson away, so you will always know where to find it.

ENRICHMENT LESSON
THE HOLY FAMILY

LESSON NOTES

FOCUS: AXIS OF THE CHRISTIAN LANGUAGE SYSTEM: THE BIRTH, LIFE, DEATH AND RESURRECTION OF JESUS CHRIST

● LITURGICAL ACTION

● ENRICHMENT PRESENTATION

THE MATERIAL

● LOCATION: FOCAL SHELVES

● PIECES: HOLY FAMILY, COLORED CLOTHS OF THE CHURCH YEAR

● UNDERLAY: FELT-COVERED CIRCULAR TRAY

BACKGROUND

We first present this lesson at the beginning of the church school year. We repeat the lesson whenever we change the liturgical colors in the room to reflect the changes in the liturgical season—purple or blue for Advent, white for Christmas, purple for Lent and so on. On those occasions, one purpose of the lesson is simple: we take the Holy Family off the shelf, change the colored cloth on the shelf to a new one, then replace the figures on the new cloth.

However, the Holy Family holds deep significance for our work throughout the year. That is why it sits right in the center of the focus shelf in the room, right behind the storyteller every week of the year. That is why we draw attention to it in this presentation to the children right at the beginning of our Church year. The Holy Family is the *matrix*—the Latin word for womb—out of which new life comes. This story is the story of the re-creation of the universe. Christ's incarnation changes everything. Most especially, it changes the way we understand ourselves, each other, the Creator and the created world around us.

We find existential meaning in our lives, in the places into which we are born, through the network of these relationships. The "answer" to life is not a propositional statement or verbal key. Instead of an answer, we find a "home," every day, in the midst of this "nest" of relationships of love and creating.

The axis of life in the Christian tradition is birth-death-rebirth. The children begin to perceive this axis through the naming of the Holy Family, and through the careful, respectful moving of the figures. We do not talk about this meaning, but wait for the children themselves to discover it. We, like the Holy Family, are invited to be co-creators in the biological, psychological, social and spiritual spheres of life.

NOTES ON THE MATERIAL

The material is a Nativity set with these figures: Mary, Joseph, the Christ child (re-movable, with outstretched arms), a shepherd, one or more sheep, a donkey, a cow and the three kings. Any size will do, but 4"- 6" works well with young children. Children can easily handle these small figures, and they won't take up as much room on the focus shelf. Behind the Holy Family, place the risen Christ with outstretched arms.

If possible, find figures that are not too detailed or realistic, so that children can supply details through their imaginations. More figures or more complex figures will not work as well as the simple set described above. Don't include a stable. It distracts from the Family.

In an ideal setup, the focus shelves stand directly opposite the door that the children enter. The Holy Family sits in the center of the top shelf. To the right of the Holy Family is the green circle with the figure of the Good Shepherd and his sheep, from the material for World Communion (see *The Complete Guide to Godly Play, Volume 4*). To the left, is a tall white candle called the Light (also called the Christ Candle). On the shelves below the Good Shepherd are the remaining materials for the World Communion lesson. Below the Light, are the remaining materials for the lesson about Holy Baptism (see *The Complete Guide to Godly Play, Volume 3*).

Below the Holy Family is a tray that contains the colored cloths of the liturgical year and a tray lined with white felt. (You will use these two trays when you change litur-gical colors during the year.) On the bottom shelf is the material for the Circle of the Church Year.

SPECIAL NOTES

Classroom management: Children can use the felt-lined tray when they work with the Holy Family, but most children will prefer to keep the figures on the top focus shelf as they move them around.

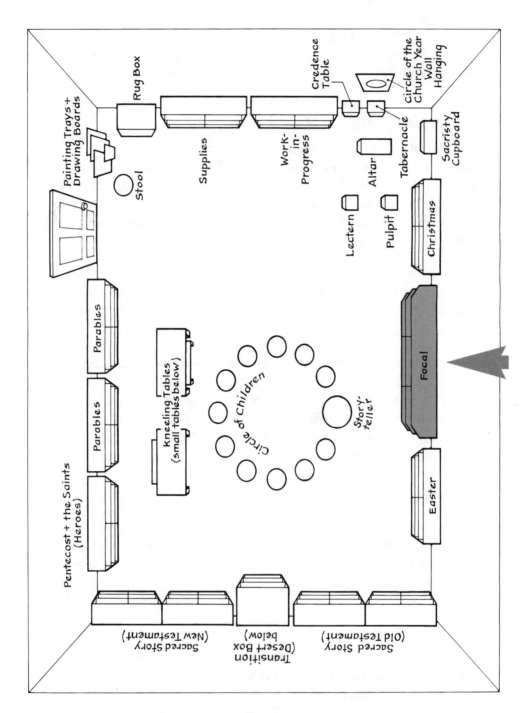

WHERE TO FIND MATERIALS

MOVEMENTS

The storyteller sits in front of the focus shelves. In the center of the top shelf is the Holy Family, which rests on a cloth colored to match the liturgical time of year—red for Pentecost, white for Easter, and so on. Behind the Holy Family, there is a picture or carving of the Risen Christ.

Tell this story whenever you change the color of the cloth underneath the Holy Family. For this fall lesson, simply have the Holy Family already placed on a green cloth. In this telling, you won't change the cloth, so you won't need the felt-lined tray. Simply describe each of the figures as you tell the story.

WORDS

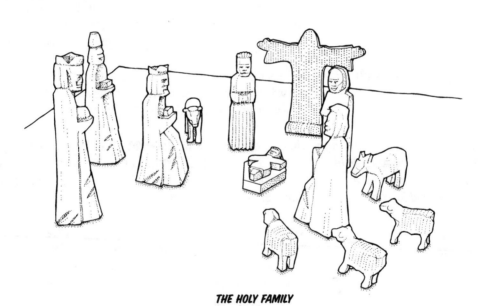

THE HOLY FAMILY

Move to the side so the children can see the Holy Family on the shelf behind you. Turn toward the shelf and open your hands to show what you are going to talk about. Wait until you are present to the story yourself before beginning.

➤ This is the Holy Family. Sometimes when you see something like this, it is not for children to touch. It might break easily, so you need to ask if you can touch it or work with it. This Holy Family is for you. It is for you to touch and work with. You don't need to ask to work with it.

MOVEMENTS	WORDS
Pick up the Christ Child from the manger and hold it in the palm of your hand for all the children to see.	This is the Christ Child. He is holding out his arms to give you a hug.
Replace the Christ Child in the manger.	
Hold Mary in the palm of your hand as well, showing her to the children. Then replace her behind the manger, looking across it to the children.	Here is the Mother Mary.
Hold Joseph in the palm of your hand and then replace him next to Mary.	Here is the father, Joseph.
Hold out the donkey and then replace it beside Mary.	Here is the donkey that Mary rode when she and Joseph went to Bethlehem to be counted by the Roman soldiers. Mary was about to have a baby, so it was hard for her to walk. Sometimes she rode on the donkey. It is also hard to ride on a donkey when you are about to have a baby. Sometimes she got down and walked.
Hold out the cow and then replace it beside Joseph.	Here is the cow that was in the stable when the baby was born. He was surprised to find a baby in the feed box, the manger, where he usually found his breakfast.
Hold out the shepherd and sheep and then replace them facing toward the Christ Child on the other side of the manger from Mary and Joseph.	Here is the shepherd who saw the great light in the sky at night. There were more shepherds than this, but we will put down one to remind us. Here are some of the sheep. There were many more, but these will do to help us remember.
	When they saw the light in the darkness, they were afraid. I would be, too. Then they heard singing. That scared them, until they heard the words. The angels sang that they came to bring peace on earth and good will to all people. The shepherds were to go to Bethlehem, and they did.
Hold out the three Magi and replace them as you speak.	Here are the three kings, the wise men. They were so wise that people thought they were magic. In their language they were called the Magi, and that word is the word from which we get our word magic. They knew so much that people thought they were magic. Of all the things they knew, they knew the most about the stars.

MOVEMENTS

WORDS

One day they saw the wild star. The Magi knew where all the stars were supposed to be in the sky, but this star was new, and it moved. This star was not on their maps of the sky. So when it moved, they were curious, and followed it. It led them to the stable where the Christ Child was.

The wise men brought with them gifts for the Christ Child: gold, frankincense and myrrh.

Pick up the Christ Child from the manger. Hold out the Christ Child to the children and continue holding him as you speak.

Here is the little baby reaching out to give you a hug. He grew up to be a man and died on the cross. That is very sad, but it is also wonderful, in an Easter kind of way.

Move the Christ Child slowly and with dignity to the picture or carving of the risen Christ. Superimpose the baby with outstretched arms on the risen Christ with outstretched arms.

Now he can reach out and give the whole world a hug. He is not just back then, in this place or that place. He is everywhere, and in every time.

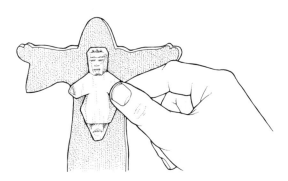

THE CHRIST CHILD AND THE RISEN CHRIST

Return the Christ Child to the manger. Sit back and quietly take in the whole scene. Be present to its meaning.

Then say:

This is the Holy Family, and you can work with these figures any time you wish. In our classroom, they are for you.

MOVEMENTS

Pause and then begin the wondering with the children.

Sit back as the wondering draws to a close. Enjoy what has been said and done. Then begin to go around the circle to help the children choose their work, one at a time.

WORDS

Now I wonder what part of the Holy Family you like best?

I wonder what part of the Holy Family is the most important part?

I wonder if you have ever seen any of the Holy Family in our church?

I wonder if there is any of the Holy Family we can leave out and still have all we need?

Now it is time to get out our work. What work would you like to get out today? You may work with the Holy Family, or you may make something about them. Maybe you have something that you are already working on. There may be another material you would like to work with. There is so much. While I am going around the circle, think about what you are going to work with.

CREATION

LESSON NOTES

FOCUS: THE DAYS OF CREATION (GENESIS 1:1–2:3)

● SACRED STORY

● CORE PRESENTATION

THE MATERIAL

● LOCATION: SACRED STORY SHELVES

● PIECES: 7 CREATION CARDS, DISPLAY RACK (OPTIONAL)

● UNDERLAY: BLACK FELT

BACKGROUND

With this lesson we begin to trace the elusive presence of the mystery of God in the story of God's People. We begin to play Hide-and-Seek with the Holy One and ask, "What can we know of the Giver by the gift?"

NOTES ON THE MATERIAL

This material sits on the top shelf of the sacred story shelves. The sacred story materials form a left-to-right sequence. For the sacred stories in this guide, the materials move from Creation to the Exile and Return. Thus the Creation material is found on the far left of the top shelf, the first material in the sacred story sequence.

A display rack holds up the seven cards so the children can see them. Also on the rack, in front of the upraised cards, is the rolled-up black underlay. This underlay is wide enough for all seven cards to be laid out side by side. The underlay is deep enough to place *two* rows of cards, one above the other. You can tape together a second set of cards to act as a self-checking set. When children work alone with the materials, they can compare their layout to the self-checking set to help them recall the order of days in creation. Store the self-checking set on a tray on the sacred story shelves, directly below the Creation material.

This lesson does not use a rug, since the material has its own underlay.

SPECIAL NOTES

At home: The days of creation make an especially wonderful story to share during a family vacation. For example, on the first day of the vacation you can lay out the first card and ask, "I wonder who saw light today?" When the family has finished sharing, you can give thanks to God for the gifts from creation you've enjoyed that day.

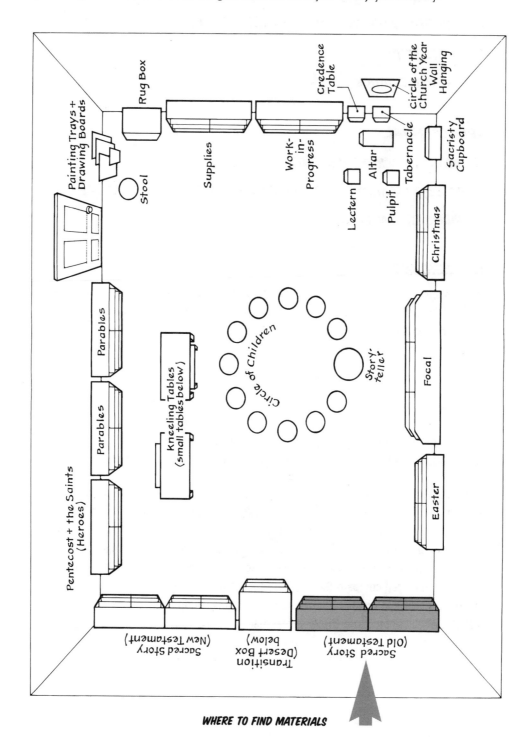

WHERE TO FIND MATERIALS

MOVEMENTS

Move slowly and with deliberation to the shelf where the creation material waits.

Pick up the display rack for the creation lesson and return to the circle.

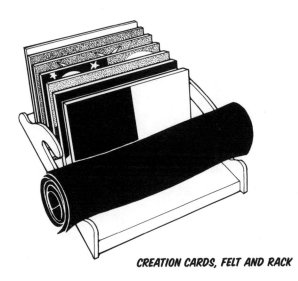

CREATION CARDS, FELT AND RACK

Place the rack beside you and get settled. Look around the circle. You may need to say:

Show the children how to "be ready" by sitting with your legs crossed and your hands relaxed on your ankles. Wait until all are ready.

Look around the circle. Smile. Invite involvement by your own sense of openness. Wait. Nod your head, "Yes," as if someone is about to speak. The grand conversation has already begun!

WORDS

➡ Watch. Watch where I go.

➡ Do you see? Yes.

➡ Everyone needs to be ready.

➡ What is the biggest present you ever got?

MOVEMENTS

The children will begin to think of things they have received. They may begin with bicycles and video games, but they also may name something alive. If this happens, comment on the distinction between a gift that is inanimate and a gift that is alive. For example, you could say:

You are not saying whether living or nonliving presents are better. You merely notice the distinction for them to comment on if they wish. Continue to affirm the children's comments.

Whatever gift that a child names, unless you sense that the child is trying to shock or disrupt the group, is "wonderful." Continue the invitation to name greatest gifts until you think that all the children who want to speak have done so.

It is not a good idea to go around the circle one at a time, taking turns. Simply acknowledge each child when he or she is ready to speak. When all who want to speak have done so, then continue:

Take the rolled-up black felt strip from the rack and place it on the floor to your right, so the children, who are facing you, will "read" the days of creation from left to right. As you speak, begin slowly to unroll the felt strip.

When the strip is unrolled completely, you move your hand across its surface to show "nothing," moving from your right to your left, smoothing out the felt in one sweep.

WORDS

➠ Listen. There's something different about that gift. (Wait to see if the children respond by describing the gift as alive. If necessary, describe that difference yourself.) That gift isn't like a bicycle. That gift is alive.

➠ Listen. Listen to your friends. These are all big gifts. They are wonderful presents.

➠ Yes. Yes. That is a wonderful present.

➠ Did you know that there are some presents so big that nobody notices them? They are so huge that they are hard to see. They are so hard to see that the only way to know that they are there is to go clear back to the beginning, or maybe a little before the beginning.

➠ In the beginning...in the beginning there was... Well, in the beginning there wasn't very much.

➠ In the beginning there was...nothing.

MOVEMENTS

From the children's point of view, you will now trace a "smile" from the children's upper left, down to the center and back up again to the children's upper right. (To you, these movements begin in the lowest right corner, move up to the center and end in the lowest left corner.)

Wait a moment and then take out the first card from the rack. This card shows the pictures of "light" and "dark."

Place the light card on the black underlay to your right so that the "dark" side of the card is closest to the right edge. Turn your hand so that the edge of your hand is perpendicular to the card and put it over the line between the light and the dark. Move your hand across the picture of light as you speak of that gift. When you name "light" or "dark," point to each.

WORDS

⬛ Except, perhaps, an enormous smile...but there was no one there to see it.

⬛ Then on the very first day God gave us the gift of light. So now there is not just darkness, but there is light and dark.

Now, I don't mean just the light in the light bulb or in the car lights at night. I don't mean just this light or that light, but I mean all of the light that is light. God gave us the gift of the light that all light comes from.

LIGHT AND DARK (STORYTELLER'S PERSPECTIVE)

As you say, "It is good," place your hand flat on the card, as if blessing it. This is probably the most important gesture in the whole lesson. Lean back, sit a moment and then begin the next day.

⬛ When God saw the light, God said, "It is good." And that was the end of the first day.

MOVEMENTS	WORDS
Place the second card to your left of the first day.	On the second day God gave us the gift of water. Now, I don't mean just the water in a water glass or the water in a bathtub or shower. I don't even mean just the water in a river or a lake. I don't even mean just the water in the ocean, or the water that comes down from the sky in rain. I mean all of the water that is water. This is the water that all the rest of the water comes from.
Move your hand across the card. You can trace the thin, white arc with your finger, or you can leave out this gesture and wait until the children ask about the line.	This is the firmament. It divides the waters above and the waters below.
Touch the card like a blessing.	When God saw the water, God said, "It is good." And that was the end of the second day.
Take out the third card and lay it to your left, so that it touches the second card. Take your time.	
Place the edge of your hand vertically on the card's line that divides the water and land as you say "divide." Move it to the right as you "uncover" the dry land. Point to the "green and growing things" on the card as you speak of them.	On the third day God gave us the gift of the dry land. God divided the water and the dry land, and gave us the gift of green and growing things.
Put your hand on the card like a blessing as you say, "It is good." Wait a moment. Enjoy all that was given on the third day.	When God saw the dry land and the green and growing things, God said, "It is good." And that was the end of the third day.
Take out the fourth card and place it to your left, so that it touches the card for day three.	On the fourth day God gave us the gift of the day and the night. God gave us a way to count our days.
Point to the lights as they are spoken of.	Here is the great light that rules the day, the sun, and here are the lights that rule the night, the moon and the stars.

MOVEMENTS	WORDS
Touch the card like a blessing as you say, "It is good." Wait a moment. Don't hurry. Enjoy the fourth day.	When God saw the day and the night, our way to keep time, God said, "It is good." And that was the end of the fourth day.
Take out the fifth card and place it to your left, so that it touches the card for day four.	
As you mention the flying creatures and the swimming ones, touch each figure.	On the fifth day God gave us the gift of all the creatures that fly in the air. Not just the birds but all of the creatures that fly. And all of the creatures that swim in the water. All of them.
Touch the card like a blessing as you say, "It is good."	When God saw all of the creatures that fly and all of the creatures that swim, God said, "It is good." And that was the end of the fifth day.
Please remember to relax and enjoy each day after it is presented.	
Take out the sixth card and place it to your left of the fifth one.	
Touch the creatures as you name them.	On the sixth day God gave us the gift of all the creatures that walk upon the earth: the creatures that walk with two legs, like you and like me, and all the creatures that walk with many legs.
As you say "all the gifts of the other days," move your right hand over all of the card. Then touch the sixth card like a blessing as you say, "It is very good."	When God saw the creatures that walk with two legs and the creatures that walk with many legs and all the gifts of the other days, God said, "It is very good," and that was the end of the sixth day.
Take out the seventh card and place it to your left of the sixth one.	

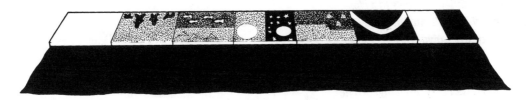

THE SEVEN CARDS (STORYTELLER'S PERSPECTIVE)

MOVEMENTS

WORDS

As you say, "all the other days," sweep your hand across the whole line of cards.

On the seventh day God rested and gave us the gift of a day to rest—and to remember the great gifts of all the other days.

Point to the seventh card.

There is nothing here, because people go to different places to remember the great gifts. You can put something there to show your favorite place to remember. It might be in your backyard by a tree, in a church or in your room. It might be in the mountains or by the ocean or a lake. I don't know where your place is. Only you know.

As you say "mark it with a cross," you can use your fingers to trace a cross on the card. As you say "mark it with a star," you can use your fingers to trace the star of David on the card.

What I do know is that this day is so special, that sometimes the Christian people mark it with a cross and the Jewish people mark it with a star, the star of David.

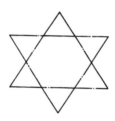

STAR OF DAVID

As you introduce the wondering questions, you can point to each card slowly as the question is introduced. For the last wondering question, you might pull one or two of the cards toward you so they are clearly out of line with the others. This is to suggest that these or others might be taken out for consideration.

Now, I wonder which one of these days you like best?

I wonder which day is the most important?

I wonder which day you are in or which one is especially about you?

I wonder if we can leave out any one of these days and still have all the days we need?

When the wondering draws to a close, turn the children's attention toward getting out their own work.

You might also explore the sequence of the days. Can they be changed? The more years you present this story, the more powerful it becomes.

LESSON 3

THE FLOOD AND THE ARK

LESSON NOTES

FOCUS: GOD'S PROMISE THROUGH NOAH (GENESIS 6:5–9:17)

- SACRED STORY
- CORE PRESENTATION

THE MATERIAL

- LOCATION: SACRED STORY SHELVES
- PIECES: ARK, ANIMALS, NOAH FIGURES, STONES, PRISM (OPTIONAL), PEOPLE OF GOD FIGURES (OPTIONAL)
- UNDERLAY: BROWN FELT OR RUG

BACKGROUND

We now move with the people of God from the creation to the re-creation and God's promise to Noah, to God's family and to us.

NOTES ON THE MATERIAL

Present this material on a brown rug or a brown felt underlay; if you use an underlay instead of a rug, it is easier for the figures to stand up. You and the children will use your imaginations to make the flooding waters as you hold up the ark higher and higher.

You also need an ark, Noah, Noah's family, four pairs of animals and several stones. Keep the animals in a basket, so you don't have to take the ark apart to get them. Keep the dove in a separate small basket; the lid of this basket becomes the dove's nest. You can also keep Noah and his family in their own basket, so they won't get mixed up with the animals and become hard to find as you tell the story. If you use a rug, find that in the rug box, which has its own place in the room. All the remaining materials for this story sit on a tray that is to the right of the Creation lesson as you face the sacred story shelves.

SPECIAL NOTES

Storytelling tips: As you tell this story, be sure to lay the animals down on the ark, or place them in another secure way. As the story proceeds, you will lift the ark up, over your head. You want the children to be able to see the animals, but you don't want the animals to fall over—or, worse, fall *out* of the ark. If an animal falls in spite of your care, simply smile, put it back in the ark and continue.

When you reach the part where the waters go down, you may want to introduce the raven (see Genesis 8:6-7) before telling about the dove. We omit the raven from the main presentation because it can be a distraction, especially for younger children. However, the raven also offers us a haunting image as we tell how it went "to and fro until the waters were dried up from the earth" (Genesis 8:7). The raven never came back to the ark for rest, but continued to search on its own until the flood waters subsided. As you begin to introduce the dove, let the raven come to rest without comment.

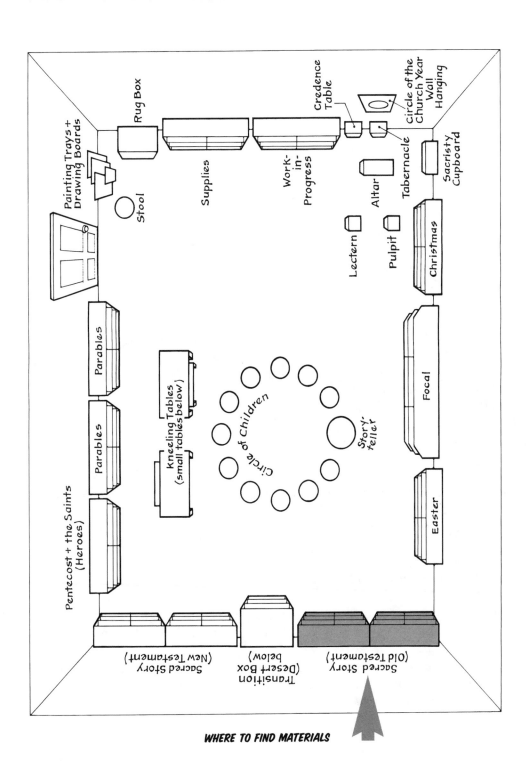

WHERE TO FIND MATERIALS

MOVEMENTS	WORDS
This lesson has a rug, so the first move the storyteller makes is to go get a rug.	⟿ Watch carefully where I go. First, we need a rug.
Roll out the rug in the middle of the circle but within reaching distance of the storyteller. Now you need the materials on the tray from the shelf next to Creation.	
Move slowly and with deliberation. You are modeling how you want the children to move with intention when they get out their work. Stop when you arrive at the shelf. Look at the children. You are keeping contact, but you are also marking this as the place where the material for the day is. There is no need to say anything if you mark this well with your action. Return to the circle and place the tray with the ark and figures on it beside you. If you use an underlay instead of a rug, spread it out now. Sit a moment and then begin.	
As you say "created everything," sweep your hand across the rug in front of you. When you say "It is very good," place your hand on the rug, as if it were one of the creation cards that was "blessed" in the Creation lesson.	⟿ When God created everything, God said, "It is very good."
Move your hand to show the water flowing across the rug.	⟿ But people began to do bad things. God decided to send a great flood of water to wash everything clean and make it new again.
Put Noah down in the middle of the rug, two-thirds of the way toward the children. Leave room for the ark, which you will place later, so that the family remains between the ark and the children. Put "Mrs. Noah" beside Noah. (Tradition says that this woman's name was Namah. In her aprons, she gathered the seeds that would sow new plants for the world.)	⟿ Then God saw a good family. The father was Noah. He and his wife had three sons, and they had wives.

MOVEMENTS	WORDS

MOVEMENTS

These two figures are enough, but you can also add three sons and their wives, in a row "below" the figures of Noah and his wife—that is, between the first two figures and the children. We know the names of the sons (Ham, Shem and Japheth) but not of the wives. Even if you use the sons and wives, you may wish to omit names, which may distract from the story.

Move Noah away from the rest of the family as he walks with God. If you only use the figures of Noah and his wife, simply touch Noah now.

Place the ark in the middle of the rug.

Place a pair of animals at each corner of the rug.

WORDS

➠ Noah walked with God. He came so close to God, and God came so close to Noah, that Noah knew what God wanted him to do. God wanted Noah to build a big boat called an ark.

➠ Noah and all of his family began to build the ark.

THE ARK WITH ANIMALS IN THE CORNERS (STORYTELLER'S PERSPECTIVE)

Move the animals, two by two, onto the ark. Lay them flat, on both the rug and the ark, so they won't fall over and distract you and the children from the lesson. For the same reason, don't put out more than four pairs of animals. When the children work with this story on their own, they can use as many animals as they like.

➠ As they were building the ark, animals began to come from all the four corners of the earth. They came two by two to fill the ark.

MOVEMENTS

WORDS

As you speak of the rain and the puddles, show the the rain coming down with your hands, moving your fingers as rain.

➠ When the ark was finished and all of the animals were on the ark, it began to rain. Water came down from the heavens and up from the earth. It rained and rained.

Move your hands on the rug to show the puddles.

➠ At first it was like any rain, but the rain kept on coming. The puddles ran together...

As the rain continues, put a hand at each end of the ark and slowly begin to lift it upward, rocking it a bit to show the motion of the water.

➠ ...and soon the water covered everything.

As you raise the ark higher, say:

➠ When the creatures on the ark looked out into the rain all they could see was water.

Finally, raise the ark above everyone—including yourself—in the story circle. Hold the ark there for a time, to emphasize the experience of submersion. Everyone who was not safe in the ark was under the water. This image recurs in the liturgy of baptism, especially in traditions that submerge the baptized person. Raising something up is also a gesture of offering we encounter in later lessons about Holy Communion.

➠ It rained and rained. It rained for forty days and forty nights.

Begin to lower the ark slowly as you talk. When it is about a foot from the floor set it down without comment. Turn your attention to the dove.

➠ But God did not forget the creatures on the ark. After forty days and forty nights the rain stopped.

Then God sent a great wind to dry up the water, and the water began to go down.

Remove the top from the small dove basket and have the lid ready to place at the far edge of the rug to your right. It will become the nest the dove makes. Hold out your hand to receive the dove, and to let it fly. Fly the dove back and forth as it searches for land.

➠ Noah took the dove. He held it carefully and then sent it forth. It flew and flew. Noah held out his hand and received the dove. There was still nothing but water.

Fly the dove again.

➠ Noah waited seven days. He sent the dove forth again. It flew and flew.

MOVEMENTS	WORDS
Point to the dove's beak and let the children imagine the olive leaf.	This time when it came back it had a fresh olive leaf in its mouth. Now there was something green and growing on the earth again.
Hold out your hand and let the dove fly forth again. "Fly" the dove around and finally allow it to settle in its nest.	Noah waited seven more days. He sent the dove out again. This time it did not come back. It found a home. It made a nest, and stayed there.
Pick up the ark again, gently rocking it. Then slowly settle the ark down on the rug.	The water kept going down, then finally the ark came to rest upon the earth.
Take the creatures out of the ark and put them in a circle. Place some stones in the middle of the circle to show how Noah "built" an altar.	All the creatures began to come out of the ark. They were so happy to be home again that they could not help it. They had to say their prayers to try to say how happy they were. They made an altar and gave thanks to God.

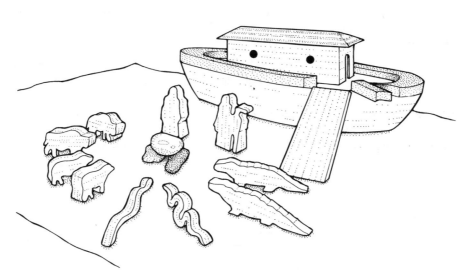

NOAH AND THE ALTAR (CHILDREN'S PERSPECTIVE)

With your hand flat, your palm facing the children, make an arc that begins at one side of the rug and goes up, then down to the other side of the rug. In other words, the arc covers the whole earth.	Suddenly, all the creatures saw a great bow in the sky. It was a bow of many colors. You can still see it today when there is rain and the sun is shining. Today we call it a rainbow.

MOVEMENTS

If you are using a prism, show it to the children now.

Move the animal pairs out to the four corners of the rug. Noah and his family remain in the middle. Wait a moment or two. You then begin the wondering.

Having the story spread out on the rug while the wondering takes place helps you and the children both. Young children who cannot yet keep a whole story in mind can see the story as they reflect. As you affirm their answers, you can lovingly touch the pieces they name. Listeners— whether children of any age or adults —can also point to parts of the story or move a piece as they try to put their reflections into words

Without hurrying, replace everything carefully on the tray. Carry the tray back to the shelf. Roll up the rug and return it.

Begin the process of helping the children get out their own work.

WORDS

➤ We can't get a whole rainbow in our room, but, if you hold this prism up to the light and look carefully, you can see a piece of a rainbow in it.

➤ This rainbow was God's sign to say that God will never send such a flood again.

➤ The creatures then went out into all the four corners of the earth and filled it up again with life again.

Now, I wonder what part of this story you like best?

I wonder what part is the most important?

I wonder where you are in the story or what part of the story is about you?

I wonder if there is any part of the story we can leave out and still have all the story we need?

➤ Now, I wonder what work you would like to get out today?

LESSON 4

THE GREAT FAMILY

LESSON NOTES

FOCUS: GOD WITH THE PEOPLE OF GOD (GENESIS 12–15, 24)

- ● SACRED STORY
- ● CORE PRESENTATION

THE MATERIAL

- ● LOCATION: SACRED STORY SHELVES
- ● PIECES: DESERT BOX, PEOPLE OF GOD FIGURES, BASKET OF STONES, BLOCKS, BLUE YARN
- ● UNDERLAY: NONE

BACKGROUND

In this story, we continue seeking the elusive presence of God. God was present at creation, blessing all that was made. Noah walked with God and was led by God's presence to build the ark that preserved life. And then?

The people living around Abraham and Sarah believed that there were many gods embedded in nature. This meant that gods had to be "here" or "there." Abraham and his family believed that God was everywhere, but was that really true? What if they were to go into an unknown place or experience, would God be there? They were not sure of this, but they put their faith in God's promises and found them to be true.

NOTES ON THE MATERIAL

This lesson uses the desert box, an important setting for several sacred stories. The desert box usually has a lid and can have wheels, to make it easy to move. If there are no wheels, place the box on a rug to drag the box from its storage location to the storytelling circle. Place the box in the middle of the circle to tell today's story.

You also need a basket with four of the People of God figures representing Abraham, Sarah, Isaac and Rebekah. Another basket holds stones to make altars. Use two wooden blocks, one about 2" x 2", labeled *Ur*, and one about 1" x 1", labeled *Haran.*

In addition, you need two pieces of blue yarn. One length will represent the Euphrates river that arcs toward Haran to guide and nourish that part of the journey. The second length of yarn will represent the Tigris River that arcs in an eastward direction.

As you face the sacred story shelves, locate this material in a tray to the right of the material for the Flood and the Ark.

SPECIAL NOTES

Classroom management: Many young children spend time in early education settings that feature a sand box. Help children understand that the desert box is *not* a sand box by consistently calling it the *desert box*. Children will almost certainly scoot up to the box to touch the irresistible sand. That's fine, but help them scoot themselves back, too. "It's time to get ready now. You need to scoot back, so everyone can see. This is the lesson."

The desert box needs an introduction whenever it is used, but be sure to spend plenty of time today introducing it to the children. Spend extra interpretive time, too, whenever you use the desert box for the first time with a new group or during a new church school year.

Take time to learn the correct placement of Ur, Haran and the two rivers in the desert box. As you move the figures correctly in the story, most of the children will see the movement as it is shown on a map. They will see the family moving from east to west, just as our biblical maps show. Your care in placing figures correctly means that children won't have to unlearn an incorrect placement of these landmarks when they learn later how to use maps of the Middle East.

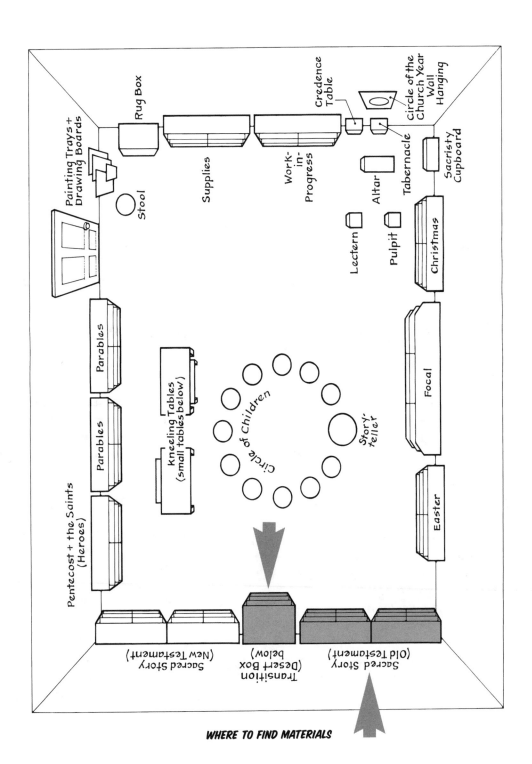

WHERE TO FIND MATERIALS

MOVEMENTS

Go and get the desert box and bring it to the circle. Leave the cover on the desert box until you are ready to begin the lesson.

Return to get the tray with the people, the "rivers," the stones and the markers for Ur and Haran. Get settled and begin when all are ready.

Trace the outline of the desert box with your finger.

Remove the lid.

As you talk, move your hand over the desert, smoothing the sand to show the mystery of the desert and what happens there.

Place the yarn and the two blocks of wood in the sand. Ur is at the left farthest from you and Haran is close to you, in the center. From the point of view of the children, Haran is at the top of a semicircle, called the Fertile Crescent. The blue yarn (for the river Euphrates) marks the semicircle.

Touch the block of wood for Ur at your far left in the desert box.

WORDS

Watch carefully where I go so you will always know where to get the desert box...

...and this lesson.

This is the desert box. So many wonderful and important things happened in the desert, we need to know what it is like.

We can't get the whole desert in our classroom, so here is just a little piece of the desert.

The desert is a dangerous place. It is always moving, so it is hard to know where you are. There is little water, so you get thirsty and you can die if no water is found. Almost nothing grows there, so there is almost nothing to eat. In the daytime it is hot and the sun scorches your skin. In the night it is cold. When the wind blows, the sand stings when it hits you. People wear many clothes to protect them from the sun and blowing sand. The desert is a dangerous place. People do not go into the desert unless they have to.

When the flood was over, the creatures went out in all the four directions of the earth to fill it up with life again. They often gathered along the rivers. The people lived in small villages and then cities. One of the most ancient and greatest of these cities was called Ur.

In the city of Ur, the people believed that there were many gods. There was a god for every tree, every rock, every flower. There was a god of the sky, the clouds, the water and the land. The world was alive with gods.

But there was one family that believed that all of God was in every place. They did not yet know that, but that is what they thought.

MOVEMENTS

Stand Abram and Sarai in the sand by Ur.

When you are moving the figures take your time. Notice how they leave foot-prints in the sand. This shows their journey.

Move the figures along the river, marked by the blue yarn, moving from your left to right, to the city of Haran. From the children's point of view, you move the figures toward the top of an arc.

Move Abram out away from Haran (to-ward the children) as you tell about Abram's encounter with the presence of the mystery of God.

Move Abram and Sarai on to your right into Canaan. As the path starts down, you will stop at two places and build altars. Then you will go down to the bottom (the farthest away from you) of the box to Hebron the final home of Abram and Sarai.

Use several small stones to build an altar.

Use several small stones to build an-other altar.

Leave Abram and Sarai together at your far right.

WORDS

Abram and Sarai were part of that family.

When it came time to move to a new place, they were not sure that God would be there. So they wondered what the new place would be like.

They walked toward Haran with their sheep and their donkeys. Even the old people and all the children went, too. They slept in their tents at night, and during the day they walked along the great river called the Euphrates. It showed them the way and gave them and all their animals water to drink.

It took a long, long time. Finally, they met people coming out from Haran. They knew the journey was almost over. Then they were there.

Sometimes Abram would go out to the edge of the desert and look out across the sand and into the sky. Then God came so close to Abram, and Abram came so close to God, that he knew what God wanted him to do. God wanted Abram and Sarai to move on again to another new place.

Abram and Sarai did what God said. They went into the desert to the west of Haran and walked toward Canaan. They went with all their sheep, their tents and many helpers. Abram's brother's son, Lot, also went with them. This time there was no river to show the way or to give them water to drink.

They finally came to a place called Shechem. Abram climbed up a hill and prayed to God, and God was there, so Abram built an altar to mark the place. Then they went on.

Next they came to a place near Bethel. Abram prayed again and God was there, also. Abram built an altar to mark this place, too. God was not just here or there. All of God was everywhere.

Then they went on to Hebron to make their home, near the oaks of Mamre.

MOVEMENTS   **WORDS**

ABRAM AND SARAI IN HEBRON (STORYTELLER'S PERSPECTIVE)

Move Abram a short distance away from Hebron. ▶ One night God brought Abram outside. He looked up into the sky. God came so close to Abram, and Abram came so close to God, that Abram knew what God was saying. "You will become the father of a great family, and Sarai will be the mother. The members of the great family will be as many as there are stars in the sky and grains of sand in the desert."

Abram laughed. He and Sarai were very old. God's promise sounded impossible, but God said to change their names anyway. Abram was to be Abraham and Sarai was to be called Sarah.

You don't need to put any figures down for the strangers. Leave them mysterious. ▶ One day three strangers came out of the desert.

Abraham was sitting by his tent. He invited them in and Sarah mixed three measures of flour, which is a lot. She gave them bread and meat to eat, and milk and water to drink, as was the custom. They told Abraham that he and Sarah would have a son, and Abraham laughed. Sarah was standing by the tent and heard them. She laughed, too. They were too old.

The three strangers went on their way. Do you know what happened? Abraham and Sarah had a son. They laughed again, so they named the baby "Laughter." In their language the word for "laughter" is "Isaac."

MOVEMENTS

Pick up Sarah and reverently hold her in your open hand. Turn your hand over and hide her as you touch the place where she was buried, not far from Hebron. Keep her concealed as the story continues.

Move your finger in the air, just above the sand, back toward Haran as you retrace the original journey.

Place the Rebekah figure in the sand, a little to your right of Haran. We won't name the place but it is Nahor in Mesopotamia (Genesis 24:10).

Move the Rebekah figure back to where Abraham and Isaac are waiting. Move the Isaac figure to meet her, then move the two figures to where Abraham is waiting. Don't hurry; this is a powerful moment.

"Bury" Abraham near Sarah by holding him in your open hand and turning it over to hide him as you touch the place where he is buried.

Scoop up a handful of sand and let it slowly trickle out.

WORDS

When the boy was grown, old Sarah died. She was was buried in the cave near the oaks of Mamre.

Abraham was lonely. He missed Sarah very much, but he had one more thing he had to do.

He sent his most trusted helper back to the land of his people to find a wife for Isaac.

Abraham's helper stopped by a well in the evening. Rebekah offered to give him some water to drink. She then helped him give water to his animals. She was as full of courage as she was kind. Rebekah then invited him home. He told her family about Abraham and Sarah and the Great Family. Rebekah decided she would like to be part of that Great Family, so they went across the desert and then past Shechem and Bethel toward Hebron.

Isaac saw them coming and came out to meet them. Then Isaac and Rebekah were married.

Old Abraham was now very old and full of years. He died and was buried with Sarah in a cave by the trees.

Then Isaac and Rebekah had children, and their children had children, and those children had children. This went on for thousands and thousands of years until your grandmothers and grandfathers had children. Then your mothers and fathers had children.

Now you are part of that great family which has become as many as the stars in the sky and the grains of sand in the desert.

MOVEMENTS

Sit for a moment reflecting on the story and then begin the wondering questions.

When the wondering is concluded, put everything away, and invite the children to get out their work.

WORDS

➭ Now, I wonder what part of this story you like best?

I wonder what part is the most important?

I wonder where you are in the story or what part of the story is about you?

I wonder if there is any part of the story we can leave out and still have all the story we need?

➭ Now, I wonder what work you would like to get out today?

LESSON 5

THE EXODUS

LESSON NOTES

FOCUS: PASSOVER OF GOD'S PEOPLE (EXODUS 11:1–15:21)

- SACRED STORY
- CORE PRESENTATION

THE MATERIAL

- LOCATION: SACRED STORY SHELVES
- PIECES: DESERT BOX, PEOPLE OF GOD FIGURES, BLUE FELT, MATZO
- UNDERLAY: NONE

BACKGROUND

God was with the People as they "went out" (the literal meaning of the word *exodus*) from slavery into freedom through the water. The People of God have looked back to this time to sustain them when God is hidden and they feel lost. For the Jews, especially, the Feast of Passover keeps alive this core event. For Christians, Baptism reawakens this event, especially when commemorated in the Easter Vigil, celebrated on the eve of Easter by some denominations.

In these stories, we continue to evoke the People's experiences of God's elusive presence. These moments of high drama reveal the complexity of such experiences and provide a narrative of their richness. This not only gives children an appropriate language to name, express and value their own experiences but also permission to talk aloud about them.

NOTES ON THE MATERIAL

Locate the tray that holds this material on the sacred story shelves, to the right of the story of the Great Family as you face the shelves. On the tray, you'll find one basket that holds the People of God and two blue felt strips rolled up separately to represent the water. Also include a basket of *matzo*, the flat bread eaten by the Jewish People at the Passover. (From now on, have *matzo* available for children to eat, if they choose, each week.) Choose one figure from the People of God to represent Moses.

The basket that holds the People of God provides the people figures for several lessons that follow (the Ten Best Ways, the Ark and the Tent, the Exile and Return, etc.). In the story of Abraham and Sarah, the Great Family became present. God's People will now journey in the lessons as they do in fact—then, now and beyond. Therefore, keep plenty of small, wooden figures in this basket.

SPECIAL NOTES

Storytelling tips: When you prepare this story, you'll find that it "telescopes" or shortens the story of the journey into Egypt for food, omitting the details of the story of Joseph and his brothers (Genesis 42ff). The story of Joseph belongs in an object box, since it is about an individual's encounter with God rather than the People's encounter. You'll find more information about making and using object boxes on pages 22 and 72 in *The Complete Guide to Godly Play, Volume 1: How to Lead Godly Play Lessons*.

Another example of "telescoping," occurs during the narrative of the plagues. Rather than list the plagues—blood, frogs, gnats, flies, animals dying, boils, hail, locusts and darkness—we simply say "many strange things happened in the land," because the list often distracts children from the primary narrative.

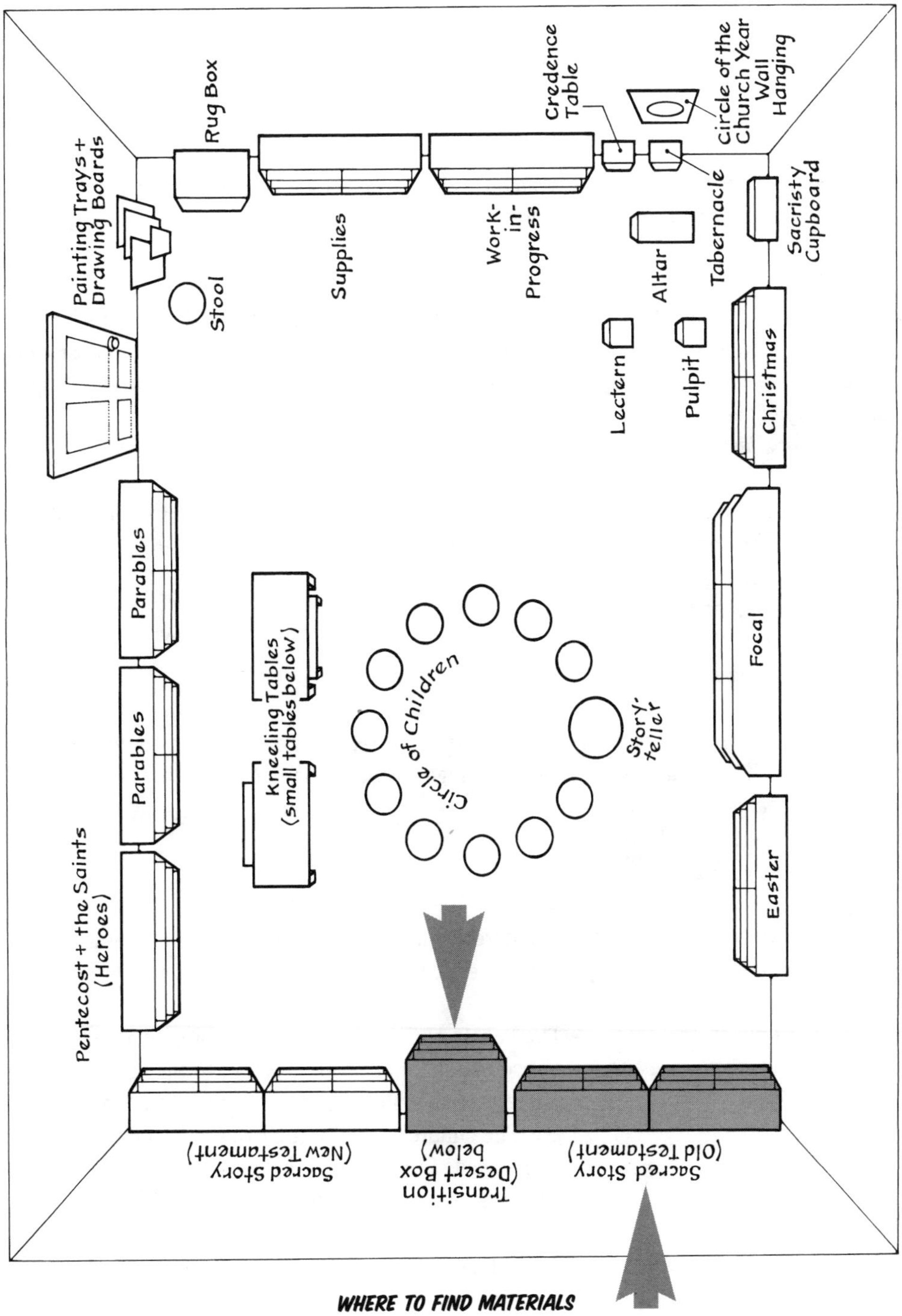

WHERE TO FIND MATERIALS

Room layout labels:
- Rug Box
- Painting Trays + Drawing Boards
- Stool
- Supplies
- Work-in-Progress
- Credence Table
- Circle of the Church Year Wall Hanging
- Altar
- Tabernacle
- Sacristy Cupboard
- Lectern
- Pulpit
- Christmas
- Focal
- Easter
- Parables
- Parables
- Kneeling Tables (small tables below)
- Circle of Children
- Storyteller
- Pentecost + the Saints (Heroes)
- Sacred Story (New Testament)
- Transition (Desert Box below)
- Sacred Story (Old Testament)

MOVEMENTS

Go and get the desert box and bring it to the circle. Leave the cover on the desert box until you are ready to begin the lesson.

When you have the desert box in place, go to get the tray with the Exodus material.

Bring the tray back to the circle and place it beside you. Now introduce the desert box to the children. This must be done carefully each time the desert box is part of a lesson.

Do not take off the lid until you are settled in the circle and the children are ready. The desert box is so exciting to some children, that you may want to wait to remove the lid until after you have introduced it.

Remove the lid. Move your hand over the desert as you talk. When you mention how the wind changes the shape of the desert, take your hand and move the sand into new shapes.

Take out some of the people and begin to place them in the sand to your left.

Continue to put people in the sand as you tell about the need to leave Canaan and go to Egypt.

Move the people across the desert, from left to right. Move them slowly, a few at a time, and reform the group several times on their way. Don't put more people into the sand than you can cover with two hands, because you will use that gesture when God's People become trapped.

WORDS

This lesson needs the desert box. Watch carefully, so you will always know where it is and how to get it out.

Watch carefully where I go. Watch. Do you see the lesson? Here it is.

This is the desert. It's not the whole desert. It is only a piece of the desert. We need part of the desert in our classroom, because so many important things happened there to the People of God.

The desert is a dangerous place. There is no food. There is no water. People die without food and water.

Nothing grows there, so when the wind blows, the shape of the desert changes. People lose their way.

The desert is a dangerous place. People do not go there unless they have to. It takes courage to go into the desert.

The People of God were living in a place where the rains did not come. The crops had no water, so they could not grow. There was no grain to grind to make bread. Everyone was hungry. The children cried in their sleep. So their mothers and fathers decided to go to a new land where there was food. They had to go even if it was across the desert. Their journey began.

It was hard in the desert, but they kept going toward the land called Egypt.

MOVEMENTS	WORDS
Move all the people to your right for their journey. This is because they will return in the next lesson from your upper right to your lower left, where you will place the rock for Mt. Sinai. When all the figures are in Egypt, pause.	In the land of Egypt the king was called a Pharaoh.
Put your two hands over the people with your fingers touching the sand.	When the people came into the land of Egypt, they found food and work, but the Pharaoh trapped them. They could not go home again.
	They had to do what the Pharaoh said. They had to live where the Pharaoh said. They had to get up when the Pharaoh said. They had to go to bed when the Pharaoh said. They had to eat what the Pharaoh said. They had to do the work the Pharaoh said. They had to do everything the Pharaoh said. They were slaves.
Remove your hands and put Moses in the sand close to you somewhere in the one-third of the desert box to your right.	One of the people, whose name was Moses, came to the Pharaoh and said, "Let my people go."
Each time the Pharaoh says, "No," hold your hand up flat between you and Moses. (You are taking the role of the Pharaoh in this dialogue.)	The Pharaoh said, "No."
	Moses went back many times to tell the Pharaoh to let his people go, but the Pharaoh always said, "No."
	Then many strange things happened in the land, but the Pharaoh always said, "No." Then something terrible happened. The oldest boy in each Egyptian family, even in the family of the Pharaoh, died.
	The oldest boys in the families of the People of God did not die, because the people made a mark on the doors of their houses. They put the blood of a lamb there, and the Angel of Death passed over them.
Hold out your hand again as if the Pharaoh is going to say, "No," but then let it crumple.	When Moses went back this time and said, "Let my people go," the Pharaoh said, "Yes."

MOVEMENTS	WORDS
	The people began to hurry to get everything ready. They packed all they could carry, and they baked bread for the journey. There was no time to put leaven in the bread and let it sit, so it would swell up and get big and fluffy like the bread you buy in the store. It was flat.
Show the basket of matzo to the children.	You can still eat this bread today. It is called *matzo*. Whenever you taste it, you can still taste this story.
Turn the people around and begin to move them from your right to your left. Move them about halfway across the desert box.	The people went as fast as they could. They were afraid the Pharaoh would change his mind. Suddenly they heard the sound they did not want to hear. The ground began to shake. The Pharaoh's army was coming after them. The beating of the horses' hooves, and the rolling of the chariots sounded like thunder!
Put down the two pieces of blue felt. They are of about equal length and meet in the middle of the desert box. Use your hand to suggest the "pushing" of the people "against" the water.	The army of the Pharaoh pushed the people against the water. They did not know what to do.
Fold each piece of felt back about an inch to make a passage through the water. Take the people through one at a time.	God came so close to Moses and Moses came so close to God that he knew how to take the people through the water into freedom.

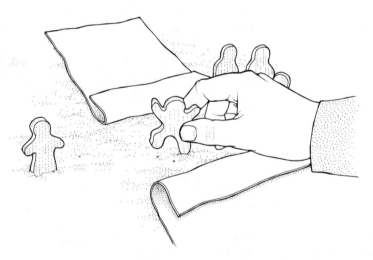

MOVING THE PEOPLE THROUGH THE WATER (STORYTELLER'S PERSPECTIVE)

MOVEMENTS

Look at the different figures and imagine how each one might feel. You might even say something like:

If there is time and the children are settled, you might pass around the basket of the People of God figures and have each child select one to bring through the water to the other side. Fold the felt back into the original position after all the people have passed through.

As the people come through the water to the other side, form them into a circle. Save one of the figures for Miriam. Place her in the center when the dancing begins.

WORDS

⮕ This one looks so scared he can barely move. This one is running. This one is happy. This one is confused.

⮕ When all the people were safe on the other side, the water closed behind them and they were free! The army of the Pharaoh could not get them.

⮕ Now all of the people were free on the other side. They were so happy they just had to give thanks to God, and Miriam led the dancing!

MIRIAM AND THE PEOPLE DANCE (STORYTELLER'S PERSPECTIVE)

Enjoy the story for a moment in silence. It is then time to begin the wondering.

⮕ I wonder what part of this story you liked best?

I wonder what part of the story is the most important?

I wonder what part of the story is about you or who you are in the story?

I wonder if there is any part of the story we can leave out and still have all the story we need?

MOVEMENTS

When the wondering is drawing to a close, pick up the basket of matzos and show it to the children.

Help the children pass the basket around and support them while they wait. When the basket is all the way around, take matzo for yourself.

Put the lesson back. Put the matzo basket on the shelf below it. Return the desert box to its place.

Begin to go around the circle to help the children choose their work.

WORDS

➧ This is like the flat bread the people made so quickly. You can still eat it today. Whenever you taste this bread, you taste this story. This is the bread of the Passover Feast. It is called "matzo."

I am going to pass it around. Every one of you may have a piece. Remember to wait to taste it until everyone is served. It is more fun to have a feast all together.

➧ That's the way. You know how to do this. Good. That's right. We need to wait. Good. It is more fun to wait until everyone is served.

Now let's enjoy the matzo all together. Taste the story. Taste how the people went through the water into freedom. You can almost taste the excitement.

Yes. There is nothing in the bread except flour and water. They had to hurry. There is no leaven in the bread to make it get big and fluffy like the bread you buy in the store. This is unleavened bread. What you taste is the story.

Watch carefully when I put this basket back. You can have all the matzo you want in our classroom. Remember to pass the basket around to everyone first. You also need to remember to taste the story.

If the basket is empty, come and get one of the teachers to fill it.

➧ Now watch. I am going to put all of this lesson back.

➧ What work would you like to get out today?

LESSON 6

THE TEN BEST WAYS

LESSON NOTES

FOCUS: THE TEN COMMANDMENTS (EXODUS 20:1-17; DEUTERONOMY 5:1-21)

- SACRED STORY
- CORE PRESENTATION

THE MATERIAL

- LOCATION: SACRED STORY SHELVES
- PIECES: DESERT BOX, PEOPLE OF GOD, HEART-SHAPED BOX WITH COMMANDMENTS, LARGE ROCK
- UNDERLAY: NONE

BACKGROUND

God was present to Moses at Sinai three times. First, God was present in the burning bush when God revealed to Moses the name of God (Exodus 3:1-6). Second, God was present when giving the Ten Commandments to the people through Moses (Exodus 19:18–20:1-17). Finally, after breaking the tablets in anger, Moses climbed up Sinai to receive the Ten Commandments a second time (Exodus 34).

On the last occasion, Moses bargained with God three times to see God's face (Exodus 33:12-14, 15-17, 18-22). But God did not allow this. No one could see God's face and live, so God put Moses in an opening in the rock and covered him until the dazzling light of God's presence had passed by.

NOTES ON THE MATERIAL

You'll use the desert box for this presentation. You'll also need the basket with the People of God figures from the Exodus story. You'll find the remaining materials—a heart-shaped box and a rock—to the right of the Exodus story materials.

In the heart-shaped box are three shapes (two tablets and a base piece) that fit together to form a heart shape. One tablet shape reads *Love God*. A second tablet reads

Love people. The third piece, the base piece, reads *God loves you*. There are also ten more tablet pieces, one for each of the Ten Commandments.

Each of the ten tablets are inscribed with a summary statement of one commandment. (See story for details.) Use dots on the back of the tablets—for example, two dots on the tablet with the second commandment—to organize this material more clearly. Finally, you need a large, rough rock to represent Mt. Sinai. To protect the wood of the shelf, place this rock on a cloth.

SPECIAL NOTES

Storytelling tips: We suggest that the story of Moses and the burning bush is part of the story of Moses' life, best told through an object box. You'll find more information about making and using object boxes on pages 22 and 72 in *The Complete Guide to Godly Play, Volume 1: How to Lead Godly Play Lessons.*

The story of the golden calf and Moses' third encounter with God are bracketed in the text for your convenience. Omit these sections, because they distract from the core narrative. However, if children ask questions about these details you will be ready to respond in narrative instead of with an explanation.

For three- to six-year-olds, use just the three summary tablets in telling the story: *Love God, Love people* and *God loves you.* Older children can hear all the commandments. From the age of nine and up, you can engage them in deeper discussion.

WHERE TO FIND MATERIALS

MOVEMENTS

Bring the desert box to the circle. Leave the lid on it. Go to the shelf and bring to the circle the People of God, Mt. Sinai and the heart-shaped box with the Ten Commandments.

Once you have the material assembled, sit and look at the desert box for a moment. If the children are comfortable and settled, remove the lid and begin the lesson. If they are not yet ready, leave the lid on and begin to talk about the desert box before removing the lid.

Put some of the people of God at your far right at the edge of the desert box. Arrange them in a circle. Also, place Mt. Sinai in the left hand corner of the desert box, the corner nearest you.

WORDS

Watch. Watch where I go to get the lesson. See? Here it is. Now you will always know where to find it.

This is the desert. It is a dangerous place. People do not go into the desert unless they have to. There is no water there, and without water we die. There is no food there. Without food we die.

When the wind blows, it changes the shape of the desert. People get lost. Some never come back.

In the daytime the sun is so hot that people must wear lots of clothes to protect themselves from the sun and the blowing sand. The sand stings when it hits your skin. The sun scorches you by day. At night it is cold. You need many clothes to keep warm. The desert is a dangerous place. People only go there if they have to.

The people of God went through the water into freedom. They were free, and Miriam led the dancing!

Now that the people are free, they can go anywhere they want to go and do anything they want to do. Where will they go now? What is the best way?

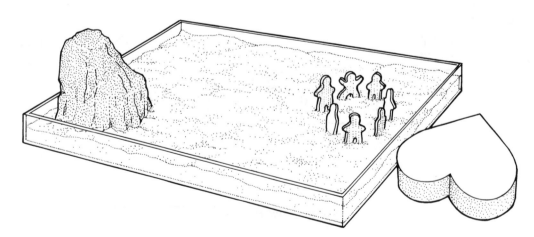

THE PEOPLE OF GOD IN THE DESERT (STORYTELLER'S PERSPECTIVE)

MOVEMENTS

Show the heart-shaped box as you say this, but don't open it yet.

Begin to move the people to your left. Mt. Sinai is in the lower left corner of the desert box, closest to you, so that most of the children can see what happens. If you put it in one of corners closest to the children, it will block the view of many of the children. Move the People carefully until they are all at the foot of the mountain.

Move Moses up to the top of the rock. As he moves up the mountain, hide the figure in your hand to show his disappearing in the smoke.

Move Moses down the mountain, revealing him from your closed hand, and place him in the sand.

[If you choose, you can add this bracketed part of the story. There is no need to make a golden calf. The children can use their imaginations to complete the scene.]

WORDS

God loved the People so much that God showed them the Ten Best Ways to Live. Sometimes these ways are called the Ten Commandments.

As the people traveled across the desert, they followed fire by night and smoke by day. They began to complain. Some even wanted to go back to Egypt. There was not enough food. There was not enough water. God helped Moses find food and water. Finally they came to the great mountain.

The People came close to the mountain, but they were afraid to touch it. Mount Sinai was covered with fire and smoke. Moses was the only one who had the courage to climb up into the fire and smoke to meet God.

When Moses was on top of the mountain, he came so close to God, and God came so close to him, that he knew what God wanted him to do. God wanted him to write the Ten Best Ways to Live on stones and bring them down the mountain to the People.

God gave the Ten Commandments to Moses. Moses gave them to the people and they gave them to us.

[The first time Moses was on the mountain, the people grew tired of waiting for him to come back. They wanted a god they could see, so they melted all of their gold and molded a golden calf to worship as if it were God. When Moses saw the idol they had made and the people dancing around it, he was angry. He threw down the two tablets of the law and broke them.]

[The next day Moses said to the people, "You have sinned a great sin." He told them that he would climb the mountain again. Perhaps God would forgive them if he went back.]

[When Moses was on the mountain, he wanted to come even closer to God's presence. He wanted to see God's face. "Show me your glory," Moses said. God said, "You cannot see my face and live."]

MOVEMENTS

[Place your hand, palm down, hiding Moses.]

When the commandments are finally presented to the people, begin to lay them out. Begin first with the summary. One tablet says, "Love God." The other one says, "Love People." A third triangular piece completes the shape of a heart, and says, "God loves us." As you lay these pieces flat in the sand, read them aloud:

Sometimes with three- to six-year-olds, it is good to stop with the summary and skip ahead to the wondering questions. With older children, you can move through all of the commandments.

As you read each of the commandments, place that tablet upright in the sand with the writing facing the children. A small number or row of dots on the backs of the commandments will guide you during the discussion.

The way the commandments are laid out is significant. There are the ones for being close to God, and the ones for being close to people, and there is one for both. It stands in the sand between the other two categories.

Place the first three tablets in a line, upright in the sand next to "Love God." Read each slowly.

WORDS

➡ [God put Moses in a cleft of the rock and put his hand over him to protect him from God's presence. God took away the hand, after passing by, and Moses saw God's back.]

[Meeting God face to face is sometimes too much for us. When we see God's back, we can follow God all our days.]

➡ Love God. Love people. God loves us.

➡ 1. Don't serve other gods.
2. Make no idols to worship.
3. Be serious when you say my name

MOVEMENTS

Read the fourth tablet and place it in a middle position in the sand since it tells us how to love both God and people.

Read the next tablets slowly and place them next to "Love People." Say each one with kindness and understanding. After reading #7 you may want to say, "You know, when people get married they think they will be married forever. Sometimes it just doesn't work out."

WORDS

4. Keep the Sabbath holy.

5. Honor your mother and father.
6. Don't kill.
7. Don't break your marriage.
8. Don't steal.
9. Don't lie.
10. Don't even want what others have.

THE TEN BEST WAYS TO LIVE (CHILDREN'S PERSPECTIVE)

I know. These are all hard. God did not say that these are the "ten easy things to do." They are the Ten Best Ways to Live, the Ten Commandments. They are hard, perhaps even impossible, but we are supposed to try.

They mark the best way—like stones can show the right path.

MOVEMENTS

Important discussions can arise from each of the "best ways" or commandments. Take your time. Wait, so children can raise issues and misunderstandings. With children about the age of ten, you may want to put two commandments such as "Honor" and "Do not lie" side by side in the sand and ask how you can keep both if Mommy or Daddy ask you to tell a lie. Another suggestion is to ask how we can keep "Do not kill" and stay alive? Almost everything we eat is alive from chickens and cows to carrots and lettuce.

When the discussion quiets down, you can begin the wondering.

When the wondering about the Ten Commandments is finished, turn back to the whole story. The story can get lost as the wondering about the Ten Best Ways takes place. It is now time to put all of that discussion back into the context of how God loves us so much that God gave us the Ten Best Ways to Live.

When all the wondering is finished, put the materials away and invite the children, one by one, to get out their work.

WORDS

▶ I wonder which one of the Ten Best Ways you like the best?

I wonder which one is most important?

I wonder which one is especially for you?

I wonder if there are any we can leave out and still have all we need?

▶ Now, let's go back again to the story. I wonder what part of the whole story you like best?

I wonder what part of the story is the most important?

I wonder where you are in the story or what part of the story is about you?

I wonder if there is any part of the story we can leave out and still have all the story we need?

LESSON 7

THE ARK AND THE TENT

LESSON NOTES

FOCUS: GOD'S PRESENCE IN THE TABERNACLE (EXODUS 25–31, 35–40)

● SACRED STORY

● CORE PRESENTATION

THE MATERIAL

● LOCATION: SACRED STORY SHELVES

● PIECES: DESERT BOX, ARK, TENT AND COVERINGS, FURNISHINGS, PEOPLE OF GOD

● UNDERLAY: NONE

BACKGROUND

There are two Hebrew words that we translate into English as "ark." One word refers to the giant boat that Noah built. The other word refers to the ark of the covenant. This latter was a box or chest that contained at least the tablets of the commandments, and, according to some traditions, the rod of Aaron and a vessel of manna.

Moses experienced God's presence on the mountain, but also in the tent of meeting. In addition, God's presence was in—or more likely seated on—a throne above the ark of YHWH. The two traditions of the tent and the ark came together in the tabernacle. The tabernacle was so important that it was described in detail twice, first in Exodus 25–31, as what, on Mount Sinai, God told Moses to make, and secondly in Exodus 35–40, as a description of what was made following the directions given to Moses.

NOTES ON THE MATERIAL

Use a desert box to present this lesson. You'll find a tray with the material for this lesson on the top sacred story shelf, to the right of the Ten Best Ways material as you face the shelf. On the tray, there is a basket that holds the ark, the incense altar, a seven-branched lamp and a table for the twelve pieces of bread.

You'll also find the tent and its furnishings: the walls of the tent, a wooden altar over-laid with bronze for sacrifices, a bronze laver for washing and four rolled-up cloths. The cloths represent the four coverings of the tent, placed on the tent in this order: blue linen (with purple and scarlet yarns and cherubim worked into it), goat's hair woven into a cloth, tanned ram's skins dyed red and goat skins as a leather outer covering.

Finally, you'll need the People of God figures used in the stories of Exodus and the Ten Best Ways.

SPECIAL NOTES

Classroom management: When you lay out this story, you won't put up all the walls provided in the material. The children, when working on their own, can build a complete tabernacle, but you will want to leave one side open, so that children can see what happens inside the tabernacle. In the same way, you won't put the four cloths completely over the tabernacle, but leave them partially rolled up so children can see into the tabernacle throughout the story.

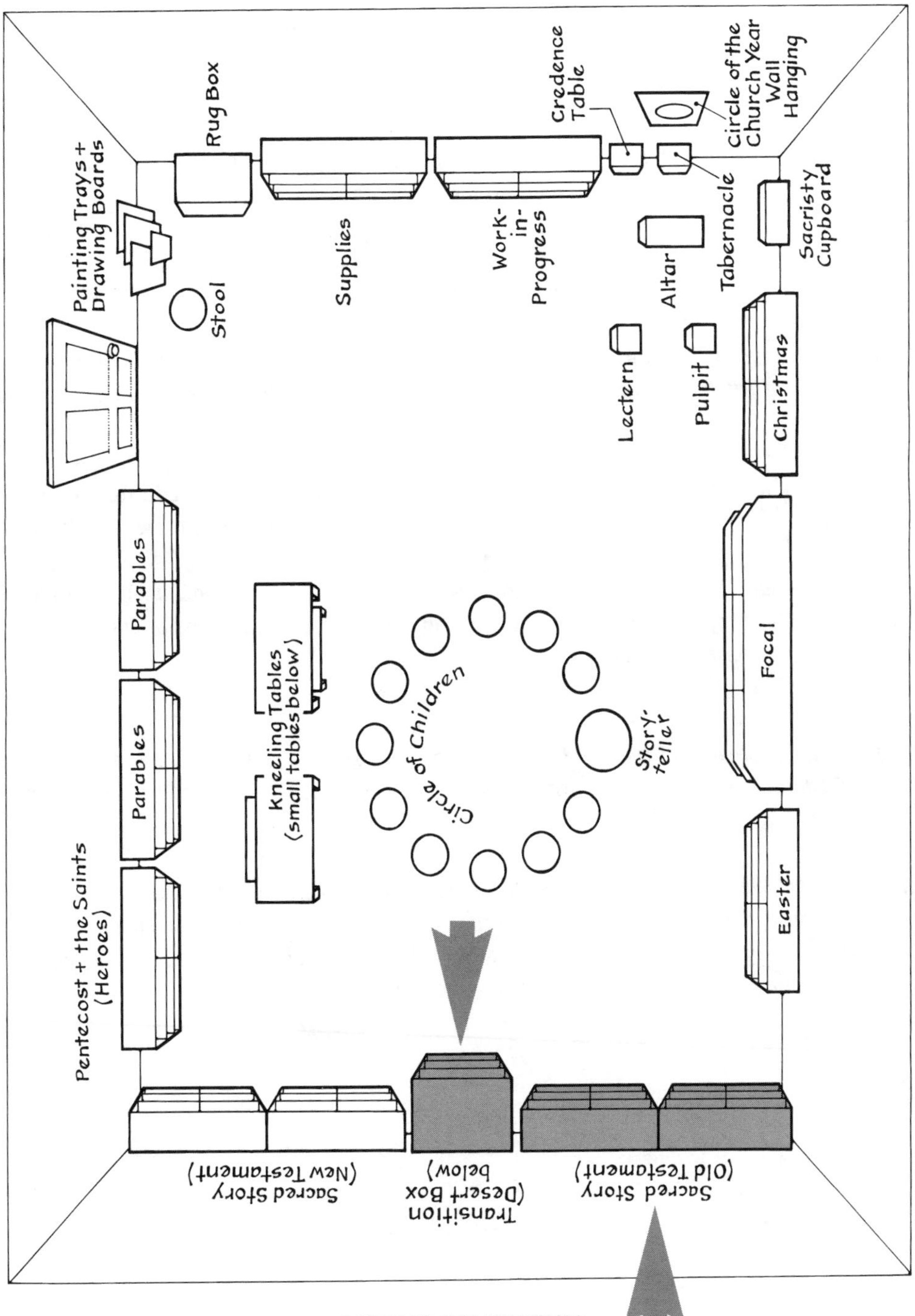

WHERE TO FIND MATERIALS

Labels on the diagram:
- Rug Box
- Painting Trays + Drawing Boards
- Stool
- Supplies
- Work-in-Progress
- Credence Table
- Circle of the Church Year Wall Hanging
- Altar
- Tabernacle
- Sacristy Cupboard
- Lectern
- Pulpit
- Christmas
- Focal
- Easter
- Parables
- Parables
- Kneeling Tables (small tables below)
- Circle of Children
- Story-teller
- Pentecost + the Saints (Heroes)
- Sacred Story (New Testament)
- Transition (Desert Box below)
- Sacred Story (Old Testament)

i wonder

MOVEMENTS	WORDS

Bring the desert box to the circle. Go to the shelves and bring the tray with the materials as described. → Watch where I go to get this lesson.

Place the ark in the middle of the desert box. → When God gave the people the Ten Best Ways to live, they loved them so much that they wanted to have them always with them. God told them to build a box called an ark to keep them in and to cover the ark with gold. It had poles on the sides, so the people could always carry it with them wherever they went.

Place one of the people in the sand and move it toward the ark, then away again. → You can't just walk up to something so precious as the Ten Commandments. You need some way to get ready. They wondered what they could do.

Put down the altar of incense to your left of the ark. → God told them to put an altar of incense in front of the ark. They could burn the incense to make a good-smelling cloud of smoke.

Move the figure through the imaginary smoke, past the altar of incense, to the ark and then move the figure back to its starting place. → You could walk through the smoke and smell its aroma. That could help you get ready. But that was not enough.

Put down the table of bread and the seven-branched lampstand. → God then told them to put a table with twelve pieces of bread on one side and a seven-branched lampstand called a menorah on the other side.

Move the figure between the table and menorah, through the imaginary smoke, past the altar of incense, to the ark and then move the figure back to its starting place. → People would walk between the table with a piece of bread for each of the twelve tribes of Israel on one side and the menorah on the other side. That could also help them get ready, but that still was not enough.

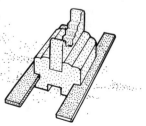

THE FURNISHINGS OF THE TENT (STORYTELLER'S PERSPECTIVE)

MOVEMENTS	WORDS
Build the fixed walls of the tabernacle, but leave open the side facing the children.	Next they decided to put the walls of a tent around the ark, the incense altar, the table and the menorah to keep this place set apart, to help get ready to come close to God's presence.
Put the wooden interior wall with a curtain to separate the Holy of Holies.	Inside the tent they made a place called Holy of Holies.
Put the four coverings over the fixed walls of the tent.	Over the roof they put four coverings. One was linen, with purple and red figures of cherubim woven into it. Another one was made from woven goats' hair. The third one was ram's skin dyed red, and finally the outer one was tanned goatskins. But that still was not enough.
Place the figure outside the tent, standing in the sand.	Now only the priests could go inside.

THE COMPLETED TENT (CHILDREN'S PERSPECTIVE)

Place the bronze altar and the bronze laver outside.	Next they put in front of the tent an altar covered with bronze for sacrifices. They also made a huge bowl of bronze that the priests could wash in to get ready for prayer, and put that in front too.
Trace with your finger the outline of a fence surrounding the whole complex.	Then outside the whole tent and courtyard they put a fence made of cloth that could be rolled up and carried with them when they traveled. It marked the whole, special area, called the tabernacle.

MOVEMENTS

WORDS

Point to the figure in front of the tent. ➧ This was not all. The priests began to wear special clothes to help them get ready to go inside this special place.

When all of the tabernacle was finished, Moses blessed it. Aaron and all of his sons were made the priests, and they took the tent and the ark wherever the People of God traveled. The Levites helped them care for the tabernacle and conduct the worship there.

God gave Aaron and his sons these words to bless the People of God: "The Lord bless you and keep you: The Lord make his face to shine upon you, and be gracious to you: The Lord lift up his countenance upon you, and give you peace" (Numbers 6:24-26).

Sit back for a moment and enjoy the whole layout of the tabernacle. Then begin the wondering. ➧ Now, I wonder what part of this story you like best?

I wonder what part of the story is most important part?

The children, especially the girls, may already have spoken out, because the boys were the only ones who could go inside the tent. If they have not, leave plenty of room and feel the permission for them to speak, but let them make the discovery and reflect on its fairness. They will.

I wonder where you are in the story or what part of the story is about you?

I wonder if there is any part of the story we can leave out and still have all the story we need?

When the wondering is finished, take the tabernacle apart with care and place it on the tray. Return the tray to the shelf and take the desert box back to its place in the room. Return to the circle and begin to help the children decide what work they will get out today.

LESSON 8

THE ARK AND THE TEMPLE

LESSON NOTES

FOCUS: A HOUSE FOR GOD (1 KINGS 5–8; 2 CHRONICLES 2–8)

- ● SACRED STORY
- ● CORE PRESENTATION

THE MATERIAL

- ● LOCATION: SACRED STORY SHELVES
- ● PIECES: TEMPLE, FURNISHINGS, SOLOMON, SCROLL
- ● UNDERLAY: USE A SOLID-COLORED RUG

BACKGROUND

When God gave the People of God the Ten Best Ways to Live (the Ten Command-ments), God also told Moses how they were to be kept. On their journeys, the people were to remember the Sinai experience by taking the tabernacle with them. The tab-ernacle complex included both the ark and the tent of meeting. Inside the ark were the stone tablets inscribed with the Ten Best Ways.

The wandering people experienced their God as nomadic and free, walking with them in unconfined, holy time. When the People of God came into the promised land, they settled down and their experience of God changed. The tabernacle was set up at Shiloh, but it was lost to the Philistines in the battle of Aphek (1 Samuel 4). The Philistines returned it, when they experienced one trouble after another. There was much sickness, and the statue of their god Dagon fell on its face!

The People of God brought the ark to Kiriath Jerim and kept it at the house of Abi-nadap who lived on a hill. The ark remained there for twenty years until King David brought it into Jerusalem, dancing at the head of the procession as it was carried into the city (2 Samuel 6; 1 Chronicles 13–16).

King David set up the ark and the tent of meeting inside the wall of Jerusalem. He wanted to build a house for God, a temple, but through the prophet Nathan, God told David that David's son would build the temple (2 Samuel 7; 1 Chronicles 17).

When the temple was finally built it reflected a new way of thinking about the experience of God's presence. God now sat in a house of cedar, built by people, thus restricting God's location. Now God was measured out to people in liturgical acts and prayers by an organization of priests. This marked a shift from conceiving of God in terms of holy time to holy space. The theology of the presence of God changed from a theology of God's name (a primarily auditory experience) to a theology of God's glory (a primarily visual experience). The nomadic transitoriness of presence becomes a cultic presence of proximity. God no longer sojourns but abides. Meeting God with openness shifts to an expanding need for certainty about God's presence.

When the priests carried the ark into the temple and placed it in the Holy of Holies, a shining cloud suddenly filled the temple with the dazzling light of God's presence (1 Kings 8:1–13; 2 Chronicles 5:2–14). God was in that place, but there is no place that can contain God. All of God is everywhere. When King Solomon prays at the temple's dedication he gives voice to this tension, but the tendency to think of God as being only in the temple will grow and distort the people's search for the true, living God.

NOTES ON THE MATERIAL

Use a rug to present this lesson. (The People of God are no longer wandering in the desert.) On a tray between the materials for the Ark and Tent and the Exile and Return, you will find the material for the Ark and the Temple. The tray holds a wooden model of the temple together with a small box containing the temple furnishings. The tray also holds a figure of Solomon, mounted on a base so he will stand up by the outside altar during his prayer. The tray also holds a rolled-up text for the paraphrased prayer of Solomon. (See the storytelling tip under Special Notes, below.)

SPECIAL NOTES

Storytelling tip: In this lesson, you read aloud the prayer of Solomon used in dedicating the temple. Write this prayer onto a scroll, and roll it up. This gives more drama to the moment of prayer in the story. The whole prayer can be found in 1 Kings 8:22–53 and in 2 Chronicles 6:12–42, but this edited paraphrase is a good compromise for the lesson.

> O Lord, God of Israel, there is no God like thee, in heaven above or on earth beneath, keeping covenant and showing steadfast love to thy servants who walk before thee with all their heart...

> But will God indeed dwell on the earth? Behold, heaven and the highest heaven cannot contain thee; how much less this house which I have built! Yet have regard to the prayer of thy servant and to his supplication... (1 Kings 8:23, 27-28a).

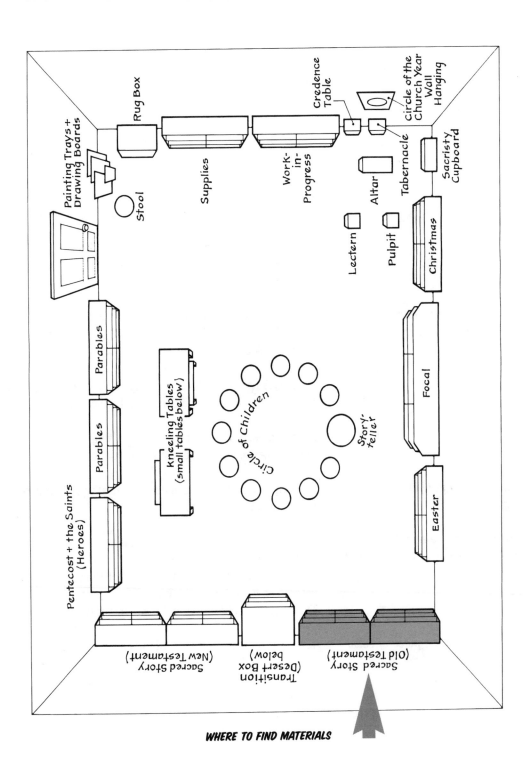

WHERE TO FIND MATERIALS

MOVEMENTS	WORDS
Get out the rug and bring it to the circle. Unroll it in the middle of the circle. Go to the sacred story shelf and get the material for this presentation.	Watch where I go to get this lesson.
Move your hand over the rug to show what it represents.	The People of God came into the promised land.
	When David became king he collected all of the people of God from the north and the south into one group. He took Jerusalem from the Jebusite people and called it the city of David.
	David and the People of God began to live in Jerusalem, but something was missing. It was the ark. David and his army went to get the ark.
Place the ark in the middle of the rug and, by gesture, show the covering of the tent over it.	When they brought the ark in through the great high gate, King David danced before it. They set up the tent of meeting and put the ark inside.
	David was not allowed to build a house for God, because he was a man of war. His son Solomon would build the temple.
	All of the people had to help build the temple. Some went to the north to Lebanon to cut down and bring home great cedar trees.
Put the base of the temple down on the rug.	They cut stones out of the mountains nearby and prepared the wood and stone to begin.
Put the pieces of the temple material together on the base as you tell about its building.	The temple began to grow, and people were amazed. There was a great hall for people to come close to God, and an inner room, called the Holy of Hollies, which was for the ark. The High Priest entered only on the Day of Atonement, the holiest day of the year. The temple was beautiful, with carvings of olive wood and gold.
Show the children the piece of cedar that covers the floor of the model.	The great timbers of cedar made it smell wonderful, like this.
Place the ark, incense burner, table of shewbread and the menorah as they are named.	Inside the temple were the same things that helped them get ready to meet God when they were in the desert. The ark was carried inside by the priests. Here is the incense burner. Fragrant smoke filled the temple as the incense burned. Here is the table with the bread for each of the twelve tribes on it. And finally, here is the menorah with its seven branches and lamps burning.

MOVEMENTS

WORDS

On the day the priests first carried the ark inside, a great cloud of dazzling light filled the temple. God was there.

Point to the altar and basin of water as they are named. ⇒

In front of the temple was the altar as it had been in front of the tent, but now it was bigger. The same was true for the great basin of water, the laver.

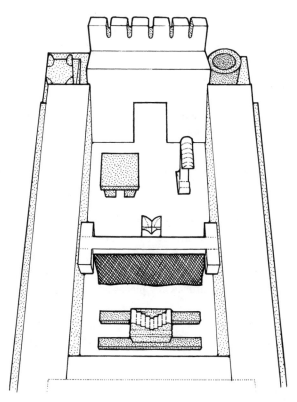

THE COMPLETED TEMPLE (STORYTELLER'S PERSPECTIVE)

Place the King Solomon figure by the outside altar for sacrifices. Unroll the scroll to read the prayer of Solomon. ⇒

On the day all was ready, the King came before all the people and prayed. He said, "O Lord, God of Israel, there is no God like thee, in heaven above or on earth beneath, keeping covenant and showing steadfast love to thy servants who walk before thee with all their heart.

"But will God indeed dwell on the earth? Behold, heaven and the highest heaven cannot contain thee; how much less this house which I have built! Yet have regard to the prayer of thy servant and to his supplication." He asked God to allow God's Name to abide in the temple. He asked God to make this the place for people to come to pray and to find justice.

MOVEMENTS

WORDS

Solomon ruled well and was wise. Some said he was wiser than anyone in the world. His father had been famous for his songs and war, but Solomon was famous for his wise sayings and the temple.

Finally, after being king for forty years, Solomon died and was buried in the city of David, where his father was buried and Solomon's son was made king.

Sit back and be silent for a moment. Reflect quietly about the story as you prepare for the wondering questions.

➮ Now, I wonder what part of the story you liked best?

I wonder what part of the story is most important?

I wonder where you are in the story? I wonder what part of the story is about you?

I wonder if there is any part of the story we could leave out and still have the story?

Sit back again. This is to introduce a special kind of wondering question.

➮ When you go to Jerusalem today, the temple is gone. It was destroyed when the People of God were taken into exile. It was rebuilt but destroyed again and rebuilt again in Jesus' time by Herod. In 70 A.D. Herod's temple was destroyed by the Roman army. Only pieces are left today.

If the temple is gone and no one can find the ark, I wonder where the Ten Best Ways are kept today?

When all the wondering is finished, put the materials away. Invite the children, one by one, to get out their work.

LESSON 9

THE EXILE AND RETURN

LESSON NOTES

FOCUS: GOD'S PRESENCE WITH THE PEOPLE IN EXILE (2 KINGS 25; 2 CHRONICLES 36:13-23; EZRA; NEHEMIAH)

- SACRED STORY
- CORE PRESENTATION

THE MATERIAL

- LOCATION: SACRED STORY SHELVES
- PIECES: DESERT BOX, PEOPLE OF GOD, CHAIN, BLUE YARN, BLOCKS
- UNDERLAY: NONE

BACKGROUND

Abraham and Sarah traveled away from their home, a land where people thought that gods were in each thing—such as in the sky, in a river or in a tree. The understanding that all of God might be everywhere sustained Abraham and Sarah as they finally made their way to Canaan, where Laughter (Isaac) was born. And God was there.

In this lesson, nearly the same arcing journey is taken by God's People, but this time in the opposite direction. Even though this journey is forced onto God's People, the same astounding discovery is made. God was not just in one place, in the temple in Jerusalem. God was also in a foreign and strange land. God's presence is not here or there, but everywhere, waiting. To be found. To find us.

NOTES ON THE MATERIAL

Use the desert box for this lesson. Locate the tray with material for this lesson on the top shelf of the sacred story shelves, to the right of the Ark and the Temple as you face the shelves. The most important item is a large chain, long enough to stretch from one side of the desert box to the other. Keep the chain in its own basket on the tray so the children can see it and wonder about it as they look along the shelves.

The tray also holds two pieces of blue yarn for the Euphrates and Tigris rivers, a block of wood to represent Haran and a larger block of wood to represent the city of Babylon, which was in fact contained within a square system of walls. You will also need several People of God figures.

SPECIAL NOTES

Storytelling tip: The People of God figures are in the basket with the Exodus material. For many of these sacred stories for Fall, you have used some of these figures. Using the same figures emphasizes that the "same people," that is, the People of God, have made this journey together, seeking the elusive presence of God.

The children also have to work out among themselves how they will share the People of God.

In this lesson, we return to using the desert box. Remember to begin the lesson by first introducing the desert box. When children are settled, you can remove the lid from the desert box. Find guidelines for helping children get ready in a circle—or helping them get ready again, after an interruption—on page 69 in *The Complete Guide to Godly Play, Volume 1: How to Lead Godly Play Lessons.*

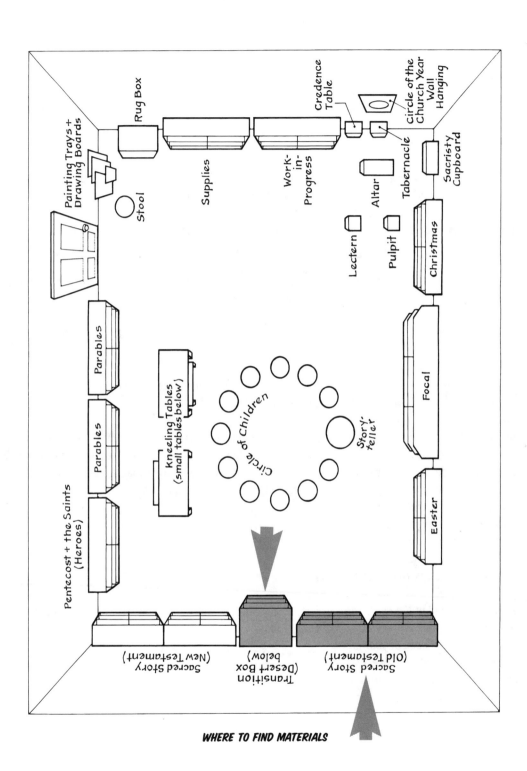

WHERE TO FIND MATERIALS

MOVEMENTS

When the children are settled, bring the desert box to the circle. Leave the lid on it. Go to the shelves and return with the tray for the Exile and Return. You will also need some People of God figures from the Exodus basket.

If the children are ready, remove the lid to the desert box and begin to tell about the desert. If they are not quite ready, leave the lid on and begin to tell about the desert before removing it.

As you begin to introduce the story, mark in the sand a square about five inches on each side in the corner of the desert box on your far right, closest to the children. Put several of God's People inside the square. This represents Jerusalem. Also mark in the sand a similar rectangle inside "Jerusalem" to represent the temple.

Place a block of wood in the center of the box, close to you, to represent Haran. Place a larger block at your far left to represent Babylon. Place two pieces of blue yarn at the left to represent the Tigris and Euphrates rivers.

WORDS

➧ Watch where I go to get this lesson.

➧ This is the desert. The desert is a dangerous place. There is no food or water there. People can die in the desert.

When the wind blows, the shape of the desert changes. You can lose your way.

The sun is so hot that people wear many clothes to keep the sun from burning their skin. When the wind blows, the sand stings your face and hands. People need protection from the blowing sand. At night, it is cold, and you need many clothes to keep warm.

The desert is a dangerous place. People do not go there unless they have to.

➧ This is Jerusalem. Here is the wall. Inside is the temple built for God. Here are the People of God. They knew that God was in the temple, but they also thought that it was the only place where you could pray to God.

➧ People thought that the wall of the city would protect them from everything.

MOVEMENTS

WORDS

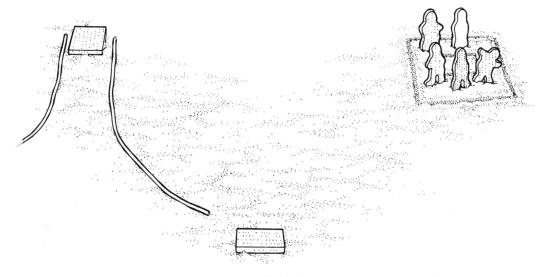

THE PEOPLE OF GOD IN JERUSALEM (STORYTELLER'S PERSPECTIVE)

Move your hand from your left to right across the desert, since the Assyrians came from the East.

Then came the Assyrians, and they attacked the city. It was a terrible time. People fought, and some starved to death. Finally, the Assyrians went away.

When the Babylonians take the city, brush the sand to erase parts of the lines to show destruction.

Then the Babylonians came, and they did not go away. Their king wanted the city of Jerusalem for himself. They broke down the walls and burned the temple.

Leave a few people in the city and begin to move the other figures away.

They took many of the people away. Only a few were left in the land.

Move the people from your right towards you and then down to your far left along the Euphrates river to Babylon. Move the figures slowly, only a few steps at a time for each figure.

The soldiers marched God's people away from Jerusalem. They looked back at the smoke of the burning city and wondered if they would ever see it again. As they walked through the desert, they had to get up when the soldiers said. They had to eat what the soldiers said. They had to go where the soldiers said. They had to go to bed when the soldiers said. They grew weary, and some died. It took a long time.

When the people pass Haran, pick up the large chain and drop it across the middle of the desert box between the people and Jerusalem. Listen to the terrible sound of the metal chain striking the sand.

They were in exile. They could not go home.

MOVEMENTS	**WORDS**
As the people approach Babylon you tell of their sadness.	They hung their harps on the weeping willow trees and sang sad songs. They dreamed of Jerusalem and the temple, but they could not go back.
Turn the figures to face toward Jerusalem.	They even faced towards Jerusalem when they said their prayers.
	Slowly, God's people began to understand that God was in this place, too. God's presence came to them as they gathered to read the scriptures, to tell the old stories and to pray
	The king of Babylon allowed many of God's People to work. They set up little stores, and some worked for the king. It was a shock when the king of Persia came with his army and took Babylon for himself.
When the people begin to return to Jerusalem, march them back the way they came and have them climb slowly over the chain, one at a time. When they "rebuild" the temple, make the mark in the sand distinct again.	This new king began to let some of the people go back to Jerusalem. Some went with Ezra. They began to rebuild the temple.
Move two or three people back the way they came and have these figures, too, climb over the chain.	More were allowed to go back. They went with Nehemiah. They rebuilt the walls around the city.
Pick up the chain and place it on the tray.	Then the People of God were no longer in exile. They could go home again. Do you know what happened? Not all of them went home.
Move your hand over the whole desert.	Now they knew God was in the strange and foreign land. Some stayed, because God was there, too.
Enjoy the story for a moment in silence. It is then time to begin the wondering.	Now I wonder what part of this story you like best?
	I wonder what part is most important?
	I wonder where you are in the story or what part of the story is about you?
	I wonder if there is any part of the story we can leave out and still have all the story we need?

MOVEMENTS

When the wondering is finished, put the lesson back on the shelf. Put the desert box back in its place. Re-turn to the circle and begin to help the children decide what work they are going to get out that day in response to the lessons and issues they need to work on.

WORDS

ENRICHMENT LESSON
THE PROPHETS

LESSON NOTES

FOCUS: THE WORDS OF THE PROPHETS TO THE PEOPLE OF GOD

- ● SACRED STORY
- ● ENRICHMENT PRESENTATION

THE MATERIAL

- ● LOCATION: SACRED STORY SHELVES
- ● PIECES: DESERT BOX, CHAIN, BLUE YARN, BLOCKS, 4 SCROLLS
- ● UNDERLAY: USE THE DESERT BOX

BACKGROUND

This lesson, especially suitable for older children, serves as an excellent introduction to lessons about the prophets, such as the story of Jonah (p. 107). We have come a long ways in time and space since creation. The People of God have been led out of slavery, ruled their own country, were defeated, carried off into exile, and returned to rebuild the temple and Jerusalem. God had been with them all the way—but they had not always been with God.

The prophets' job was to show the people, the king and the priests when they turned away from God. When the prophets communicated what God told them, they might use words, or they might act out God's message in dramatic ways. Jeremiah put a yoke on his own neck and walked about the streets of Jerusalem to show the people that would become captives. The priests understood the message and smashed the yoke.

In Jeremiah 18:18, the people say that priests teach and wise men give advice, but the prophet speaks the "word" or message of God. A secular messenger of those times, who spoke on behalf of a king, used traditional messenger-speech, first naming the one spoken for, then using the first-person voice to recite the message. Prophets spoke the same way: they identified themselves as speaking for God, then spoke "with God's voice" on behalf of God to the audience God had chosen for the message.

The role of prophets changed over time in Israel. In ancient Israel, a judge was like a priest, a ruler and a prophet all in one person. After Samuel anointed Saul, kings began to rule. The priests led the people in worship. At that time, prophets arose to challenge the kings, the priests and the people. After the exile there were no more independent kings, and the priests needed support to help the people keep their identity. The role of the prophets was absorbed into the role of the priest.

NOTES ON THE MATERIAL

Use the desert box to present this lesson. You'll again use material from earlier stories: the blocks representing Haran and Babylon and the large chain from the story of the Exile and Return. As you face the sacred story shelves, you'll also find one special material for this story on the top shelf, to the right of the material for the story of the Exile and Return. This special material is a basket with four scrolls: the scroll of the twelve minor prophets, the Isaiah scroll (that represents the writings of three Isaiahs), the Jeremiah scroll and the Ezekiel scroll.

SPECIAL NOTES

Storytelling tip: There were many prophets named in the Old Testament, but this lesson will tell about only a few to give the children an idea of what prophets do. These prophets, as well as prophets not mentioned here, can be more fully explored by using object boxes. For more information on making and using object boxes, see pages 22 and 72 in *The Complete Guide to Godly Play, Volume 1: How to Lead Godly Play Lessons.*

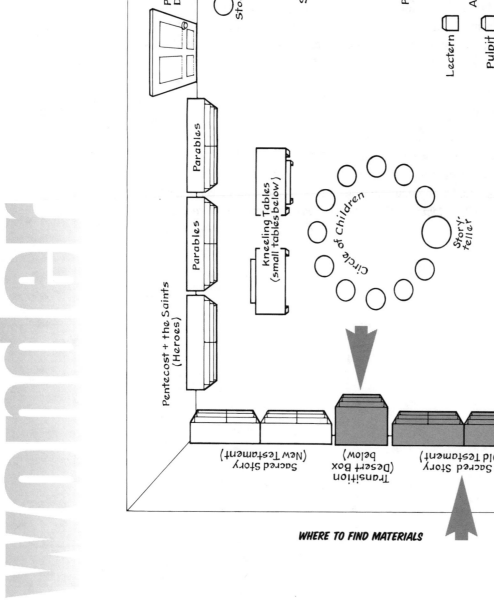

WHERE TO FIND MATERIALS

MOVEMENTS	WORDS
Get the desert box and place it in the middle of the circle.	Watch carefully where I go, so you will always be able to find this lesson.
Bring to the circle the basket with the materials for the Exile and Return. Place it beside you.	Keep looking. I am not finished yet.
Bring the basket of four scrolls and place it on the other side of where you are sitting.	
As you begin to introduce the story, mark in the sand a square about five inches on each side in the corner of the desert box on your far right, closest to the children. This represents Jerusalem.	This is Jerusalem. Here is the wall. This was the city of David, the city of the People of God.
Place a block of wood in the center of the box, close to you, to represent Haran. Place a larger block at your far left to represent Babylon. Place two pieces of blue yarn at the left to represent the Tigris and Euphrates rivers.	Here is Haran and here is Babylon.
Now you are ready to begin.	Sometimes the People of God forget who they are. They hide from God, and pretend that God isn't there. Sometimes they even worship other gods.
	There are also people who come so close to God, and God comes so close to them, that they know what God wants them to say or do. These people are called prophets. They know the best way. Both men and women are prophets, so both boys and girls can be or grow up to be prophets.
	After King Solomon died, his kingdom was divided into two parts. A prophet named Ahijah showed that God knew this was the best way. He took off his new cloak and cut it into twelve pieces.
Point to the corner of the desert box on the far right, close to you, to show the northern kingdom. Then point to the rectangle you have traced in the sand for Jerusalem, the capital of the southern kingdom.	Ten pieces were for the tribes that were around the city of Samaria, the capital of the Northern Kingdom, and two pieces were for the tribes around Jerusalem, the capital of the Southern Kingdom.

MOVEMENTS	WORDS

WORDS

Some prophets, like Elijah and Elisha, left none of their own words. They were either lost or never written down. Others wrote down what God told them to say, or some of their friends wrote down their words.

Show the basket of scrolls.

➡ I want to show you something about the ones who left their words for us. The words are on four scrolls. Here are four small scrolls to help us remember.

Pick up each scroll named to show to the children.

➡ This one is very interesting. It has the writing of twelve prophets on it. This one is called Isaiah, but it really has the writing of three Isaiahs on it. This one is all the words of Ezekiel, and this other one is all the words of Jeremiah.

Point away from yourself, in the direction of Jerusalem traced in the sand.

➡ Now let's see what happened. Here is the southern kingdom.

Open the scroll of the twelve minor prophets to read these words from Amos, together with the names of the prophets on the scrolls.

➡ A prophet who spoke to them is Amos. I will put the scroll of the twelve prophets there to remind you. Let me read something from the scroll:

> "I hate, I despise your feasts,
> and I take no delight in your solemn assemblies.
> Take away from me the noise of your songs;
> To the melody of your harps I will not listen.
> But let justice roll down like waters,
> And righteousness like an ever-flowing stream."
> (Amos 5:21, 23-24)

Amos spoke for God to the priests and to the king. This is what all the prophets did.

Now here are the names of all the prophets on that scroll: Hosea, Joel, Amos, Obadiah, Jonah, Micah, Nahum, Habakkuk, Zephaniah, Haggai, Zechariah and Malachi.

Roll up the scroll of the twelve and place it between you and Jerusalem.

One day, the southern kingdom was conquered by Assyria. Then the Assyrians surrounded Jerusalem. The people were afraid, but the Assyrians went away.

MOVEMENTS

Put the Isaiah scroll down by Jerusalem.

As in the story of the Exile and Return, pick up the large chain and drop it across the middle of the desert box between Babylon and Jerusalem. Listen to the terrible sound of the metal chain striking the sand.

Move the scroll of Isaiah from Jerusalem to Babylon.

WORDS

➧ Isaiah of Jerusalem said that the kingdom would fall, but that a remnant, a few of the people, would be saved.

It was not the Assyrians but the Babylonians who took the city, and they took many people away into exile.

➧ The second Isaiah must have been one of those people who was taken, and he wrote his words in Babylon.

He said there would be a highway, made straight in the desert, that they would go home one day. He was hopeful.

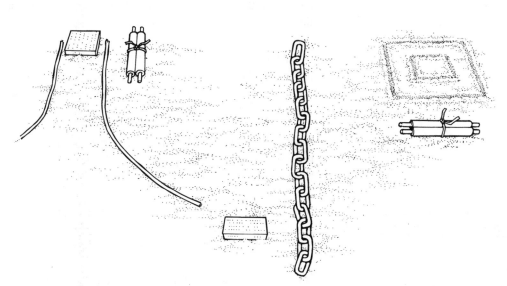

THE CHAIN AND THE SCROLLS OF ISAIAH AND THE TWELVE MINOR PROPHETS (STORYTELLER'S PERSPECTIVE)

Move the scroll of Isaiah from Babylon back to Jerusalem.

➧ The third Isaiah was one of the people who went back to Jerusalem. The people there were not really glad to see him and the others who returned. The city was still broken down. Many of the walls were still black from the fires the Babylonians had set. This Isaiah helped the people and the priests get ready for a time when they would not have their own king.

MOVEMENTS

WORDS

Put the Jeremiah scroll down by Jerusalem.

➡ Jeremiah stayed in Jerusalem. He said that the city would fall, but that the people of Jerusalem would not understand what he was talking about.

Finally, when the Babylonians came, he and Baruch, his scribe, went to Egypt with some others to be safe. But he was very sad.

Put the Ezekiel scroll down by Jerusalem.

➡ Ezekiel wrote in Babylon. He was taken away with one of the first groups, even before Jerusalem was torn down. He was a prophet in his new home.

He told the people in exile that Jerusalem would be destroyed, and that they would not go home soon. After Jerusalem was destroyed, he had visions of hope that they would go home again. They would be like dry bones in a valley that put themselves back together again, turned into people and walked to their old home.

These are most of the prophets in the Old Testament. We know a lot about them because their words were written down a long time ago.

Today there are still prophets. They speak to the rulers, to the priests, the ministers and rabbis, and to the people. They still say and do what God wants them to. They help all of us know the true way to live and die.

Prophets come from all kinds of places and are all kinds of people—just like you. So some of you in this circle may be or become prophets.

Sit quietly and reflect on the scene for a few moments. Then begin the wondering.

➡ Now I wonder what you like best about the prophets?

I wonder what's most important about the prophets?

I wonder if you know any prophets, or if any prophets know you?

I wonder if the prophets in the Bible are all the prophets we need?

Gather up the scrolls and place them in the basket. Gather up the other materials and place them in the basket for the Exile and Return. Put the baskets back and then roll the desert box back to its place. Return and sit quietly for a moment, then help children, one at a time, choose their work.

JONAH, THE BACKWARD PROPHET

LESSON NOTES

FOCUS: THE PROPHET JONAH (JONAH 1-4)

- **SACRED STORY**
- **ENRICHMENT PRESENTATION (OBJECT BOX)**

THE MATERIAL

- **LOCATION: SACRED STORY SHELVES**
- **PIECES: BOAT, NINEVEH MODEL OR BLOCK, JONAH, BROWN FELT (LAND), GREEN "PLANT," WOODEN SEA-STRIPS, CLEAR PLASTIC OBJECT BOX**
- **UNDERLAY: BLUE FELT**

BACKGROUND

It was probably after the Exile, when Judah was still under the rule of the Persians, that someone wrote a funny, entertaining, thought-provoking story about the prophets. The story shows that the spirit of God's People was still alive, still creative and still pondering the presence of the mystery of God.

This ironic tale shows Jonah, "the backward prophet," doing everything wrong, yet everything comes out right except, perhaps, his own relationship with God. The story leaves us with many questions, and we are left to finish the story for ourselves. What happened to Jonah next?

NOTES ON THE MATERIAL

As you face the sacred story shelves, look at the shelf underneath the stories of the Exile and Return and the Prophets to find the object box about Jonah. If you have other object boxes about the lives of individual prophets, the box about Jonah will be found in that group.

Inside the box are a boat, a model of Nineveh (or a wooden block representing Nineveh), Jonah, a fish, a green plant (made of felt or other material), blue wooden sea-strips to represent the waves, a blue felt sea (the underlay) and a brown felt land.

SPECIAL NOTES

Classroom management: You can find more information on object boxes and how to use them on pages 22 and 72 of *The Complete Guide to Godly Play, Volume 1: How to Lead Godly Play Lessons.*

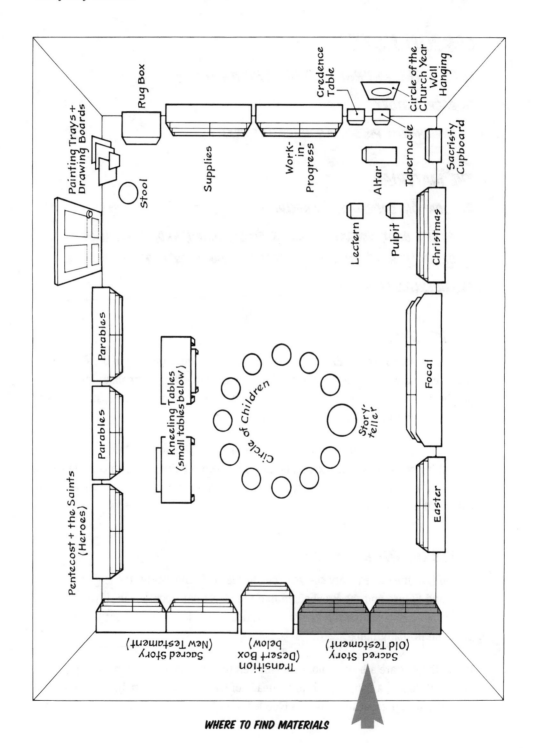

WHERE TO FIND MATERIALS

MOVEMENTS

Go get the object box with the material in it. Bring it to the circle. Lay out the blue underlay in front of you. Put the brown shoreline over it at your left. Put the model of Nineveh on the brown felt, to your near left, so it will be "northeast" of the sea from the children's point of view. (When they look at a map as they grow older, they will not have to relearn the geography.) Put the Jonah figure midway from the top and bottom on the land. Place the boat half in the water, near Jonah.

WORDS

Watch where I go to get this lesson.

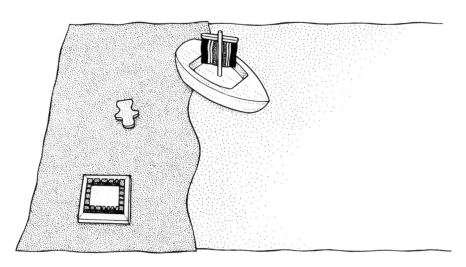

NINEVEH, JONAH AND THE BOAT (STORYTELLER'S PERSPECTIVE)

Wait a moment until all are ready. Begin with some drama.

Point to the model of Nineveh to the east (your left) as you speak.

Now the word of the Lord came to Jonah. "Arise, go to Nineveh, that great city, and tell them they are bad and they need to change and become good."

Now prophets are people who come so close to God, and God comes so close to them, that they know what God is telling them to do. Then they go do it.

MOVEMENTS

Put Jonah in the boat and push off. Begin to sail toward the west end of the Mediterranean Sea (to your right).

Place the blue wooden strips around the boat and put the prow of the boat on one of them to show how the boat is being tossed.

WORDS

➧ Jonah turned and went the other way. He found a ship going to Tarshish in Spain. It was as far from Nineveh as you could go.

➧ Suddenly a great storm broke out.

The sailors were afraid, so each one prayed to his own god. They threw everything they were carrying into the ocean to make the ship light, so they could float.

Now a prophet is someone who helps people discover what is best to do.

They went to look for Jonah. Do you know where he was? He was asleep in the bottom of the boat. The captain found him and commanded him to call on his God to save them.

All Jonah did was climb up onto the deck of the boat.

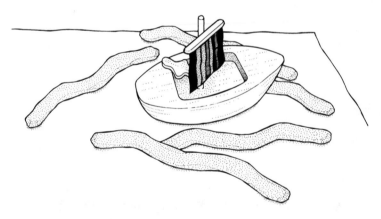

JONAH AND THE STORM (STORYTELLER'S PERSPECTIVE)

Now people were more afraid. They decided to cast lots to see whom God was angry at. They wanted to throw that person overboard to get rid of him.

Now a prophet is someone who can speak for the One True God, but Jonah still did not speak. The sailors asked him who he was. He told them he worshiped God, the One who made the sea and the dry land. Then the sailors were afraid. They knew that he was trying to flee from God.

MOVEMENTS	**WORDS**

The sea grew even more troubled, so Jonah said, "Throw me in, and the storm will stop."

Throw Jonah into the water and move the boat away from him slowly. ➡ So they threw him in. All was suddenly quiet. The sea was calm.

Now a prophet is someone who brings people close to God by what he or she says and does. Jonah said nothing; but when the sea grew calm the sailors all fell down and worshiped the true God.

Now a prophet is someone who is close to God, and a false prophet is very far from God. When Jonah was thrown into the water, he was neither close to nor far from God. He was sinking.

Move the fish across the blue felt and scoop up Jonah into the fish's mouth. ➡ As he sank, a great fish swam up and swallowed him.

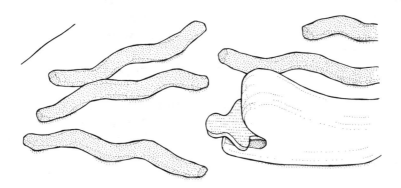

JONAH AND THE FISH (STORYTELLER'S PERSPECTIVE)

Move the fish around slowly in circles. ➡ Jonah was in the belly of the whale for three days and three nights.

Jonah began to pray and the fish began to feel very strange. It grew sicker and sicker.

Move the fish toward the land and flip Jonah out onto the land. ➡ Finally it swam to the shore and vomited out Jonah onto the dry land.

Move Jonah toward the model of Nineveh. ➡ Now the word of the Lord came to Jonah a second time. "Arise, go to Nineveh, that great city, and tell the people there that they are bad and that they need to change and become good."

This time Jonah went to Nineveh.

MOVEMENTS	WORDS
	He cried out to the people of Nineveh that they were bad and that God commanded them to be good. God said that they would all be destroyed if they did not.
	Now a prophet is someone who is overjoyed when people who are bad become good.
	The people of Nineveh listened to God's call and they turned and became good. All went about wearing sackcloth and ashes to show how sorry they were. Even the king and queen were sorry and became good. The creatures in the field were sorry too, and they also became good.
	God did not destroy that great city.
Move Jonah a little bit away from the city. Have the green plant ready to place over Jonah as he sits and sulks.	This made Jonah angry. He wanted God to destroy the city. These people were not even the People of God! He went outside the city and sat on a hill and sulked. He wanted to get his way. God said, "Why are you angry?"
	God caused a plant to grow and give Jonah shade as he sat on the hill in the sun. Then one night God sent a worm to attack the plant. It withered away and died. When the sun rose, a sultry east wind came, and the sun beat down on the head of Jonah so that he was faint. He grew angry about the death of the plant.

JONAH AND THE PLANT (STORYTELLER'S PERSPECTIVE)

MOVEMENTS

WORDS

"Why are you angry about the plant?" God asked. Jonah said, "I am angry—angry enough to die." He thought he still might get his way.

God said, "You pity the plant, but you did nothing for it. You did not cause it to grow. You did not care for it. Should I not pity Nineveh, that great city where there are more than 120,000 people, and all their cattle?"

Sit up and lean back. Reflect silently for a moment. Then, begin the wondering.

➤ I wonder what part of the story you like best?

I wonder what part of the story is the most important part?

I wonder where you are in the story? What part of the story is about you?

I wonder if there is any part of the story we can leave out and still have all the story we need?

If the children pick up this question, go with it, using the extra wondering questions provided. They may not want to work with it yet. If they do not, conclude the first set of wondering questions and come back to these additional questions another time.

➤ I wonder how you would finish the story?

What did Jonah say? What did he do next?

Put everything back in the box without hurrying. Replace the box on the shelves and guide the children's choices about getting out what they need for their responses or the other materials they might like to work with.

ENRICHMENT LESSON
THE BOOKS OF THE BIBLE

LESSON NOTES
FOCUS: CONNECTING GODLY PLAY LESSONS TO THE WRITTEN BIBLE

● SACRED STORY

● ENRICHMENT PRESENTATION (SYNTHESIS)

THE MATERIAL

● LOCATION: SACRED STORY SHELVES

● PIECES: WOODEN BOOK SHELF, WOODEN BIBLE "BOOKS," CONTROL KEY, SUMMARY CARDS

● UNDERLAY: NONE

BACKGROUND

This is a synthesis lesson for the entire Bible, especially the sacred stories. In it, we focus on both the individual books of the Bible and the kinds of writing included in the Bible.

This material is an aid to learning the books of the Bible, but in Godly Play the contents of the books, the genres they represent, and where you can find the related teaching objects in the room are also involved. You can enrich the room with materials related to this lesson. For example, you notice that much of the New Testament is made up of letters. What does this mean? You go to the New Testament shelves and find the lesson on Paul's Discovery (*The Complete Guide to Godly Play, Volume 4*, Lesson 14, pp.126-135) on the top shelf. Below there is a basket of small scrolls, each one a summary of one of Paul's letters.

NOTES ON THE MATERIAL

The material for this lesson is a small wooden bookshelf with wooden "books," each labeled with the title of one book of the Bible. Provide one wooden "book" to represent each book of the Bible. Use color coded titles to organize the "books" into types of writing, such as the Law (5 books), the gospels (4 books), Old Testament history (11 books), Paul's letters (13 books), and so on.

The material includes a control key, such as a poster, that shows the colors and a list of the books in each of the groups. Locate the control key on the back of the bookshelf to help teach the lesson. The material also includes color-coded summary cards, with one or two sentences about the content of each book. (For example: "Jonah—This book was written after the Exile of Israel. In this story, the prophet Jonah does everything wrong—but somehow things still come out all right.")

In front of the shelf and the basket of summary cards, keep a Bible on a stand. Before each lesson, open this Bible to the lesson for the day.

SPECIAL NOTES

Art project: Throughout the year, invite children to make bookmarks that represent the day's lesson. Even nonreaders can make creative bookmarks!

Place these bookmarks in the Bible at the appropriate places. When the worship-education year begins, the Bible is empty, but by the end of the year the children will fill it with markers that link the lessons in the room to the Bible as a book.

MOVEMENTS

When the children are ready, go to the shelf and bring the Bible on its stand, the basket with the summary cards and the bookshelf with books.

Place the bookshelf with the books and the basket beside you. Put the Bible on its stand in front of you, facing the children.

WORDS

Watch where I go. Remember to carry the Bible with two hands. Be careful. Here is the basket of summary cards. You may need someone to help you carry the little books and bookshelf. Carry the bookshelf flat, so the little books won't fall out.

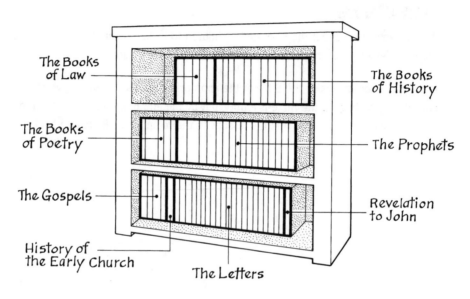

The Books of Law

The Books of History

The Books of Poetry

The Prophets

The Gospels

Revelation to John

History of the Early Church

The Letters

THE BOOKS OF THE BIBLE (CHILDREN'S PERSPECTIVE)

Pick up the book and look at it with respect and pleasure, then put it back on its stand.

This is the Holy Bible. It wasn't always a book. A long, long time ago it was stories around campfires in the desert and later in peoples' homes.

Then the stories were written down on pieces of soft leather, then on a kind of paper made from reeds called papyrus.

Pick up the Bible again.

Finally the printing press was invented and the Bible became a book.

Open the front and back covers of the book.

Here is the front door and here is the back door. Here we open up both doors and let the stories out! They are all over our classroom. We still tell them in a circle, like around a campfire. Sometimes parts of the Bible are in a video or movie, but here we still like to tell them the old, old way.

MOVEMENTS

Pause and then move the bookshelf in front of you between you and the Bible, facing the children.

Count the books and compare the Old and New Testaments.

Read the different kinds of books.

Use the control key to show the different kinds of books and describe what they are.

Get the basket of summary content cards. Show how the control key and summary cards work together so they can check their own work. Pick a card at random from the basket, then show where it is in the "library" and tell what it is about.

Pick a book you know—for example, Genesis—to show what on the story shelves is from Genesis. Get up with the little book and hold it next to the stories that it contains.

Return to the circle and sit down. Put your hand on the bookshelf.

Point to the Law section. Lay out the books and recite them from memory.

WORDS

Look at all the books in the Bible. The Bible is like a whole library! Let's count the books in the library.

There are different kinds of books, too. See?

Here is a control card, so you can check your own work. Try taking out a little book and putting it back in the library, in the right place. What kind of writing is it?

I have an idea. Let's figure out what the books are about. You might want to read one sometime, so we need to know where they are and what they are about.

We also want to know what is in our classroom from each book. Let's put the little book beside each story it includes, and then put it back on its shelf.

See, here they are. The Creation is from Genesis. The Flood and the Ark is too. The Great Family also belongs there. The first three stories on our Sacred Story shelf are all from the first book of the Bible.

You know, some people even memorize the books of the Bible, so they can carry their names with them all their days. Knowing the order of the names also helps you find things in the Bible faster. You know your way around.

You can memorize the books in small bits while you are learning about them. This is how it works. See the part called the Law? There are only five books. They are Genesis, Exodus, Leviticus, Numbers, Deuteronomy. That's not so hard, is it?

MOVEMENTS	WORDS
Enjoy the whole bookshelf. Touch several of the books with wonder.	⟶ Now, I wonder which one of the books you like best?
	I wonder which one is the most important one?
	I wonder which one is especially for you?
	I wonder if there are any books we can leave out and still have all the books we need?
Point to the kinds of books—Law, Gospels, History, Paul's Letters, etc.	⟶ Now, I wonder which kinds of books you like best?
	I wonder which kind of book is the most important?
	I wonder which kinds of books are especially for you?
	I wonder if we can leave out any of the kinds of books and still have all the kinds we need?
Replace all of the materials on the shelf. Help the children choose their work.	⟶ I wonder what work you would like to get out today?